Tread the City's Streets Again

Frances Perkins Shares Her Theology

Donn Mitchell

Anglican Examiner Publications
Princeton
2018

Anglican Examiner Publications
126 John St.
Princeton, NJ 08542

Tread the City's Streets Again: Frances Perkins Shares Her Theology
ISBN 978-1-64254-712-2

To my mother,

June Bishop Mitchell,

whose love of the New Deal

inspired my own.

St. Thomas, Fifth Avenue, where Frances Perkins shared the theology of her vocation as part of the St. Bede Lectures of 1948.

Table of Contents

*Loving God, we bless your name for
Frances Perkins, who lived out her
belief that the special vocation of the
laity is to conduct the secular affairs of
society that all may be maintained in
health and decency.*

*Help us, following her example, to
contend tirelessly for justice and for the
protection of all in need, that we may
be faithful followers of Jesus Christ,
who with you and the Holy Spirit lives
and reigns, one God, forever and ever.
Amen*

Collect for the Feast of Frances Perkins, May 13
Holy Women, Holy Men (Church Publishing 2010)

Preface

The New Deal was the longest presidential administration in U.S. history. The consensus it forged dominated U.S. politics from 1932 to 1980, producing the closest thing to social democracy the United States has ever seen. Frances Perkins, the heart and soul of New Deal social policy, made history as the first woman to be appointed to a Presidential Cabinet. But it is not for this reason alone that the Episcopal Church has added her to its calendar of saints. May 13 has been set aside to commemorate a life of profound service to humanity, motivated by a steadfast faith in Jesus Christ.

Perkins was a committed, theologically articulate Episcopalian, steeped in the incarnational emphases of Anglo-Catholic socialism, a movement within Anglicanism that was especially strong during her lifetime. This movement will be explained in more detail in Chapter One.

In addition to being a lay associate of All Saints Sisters of the Poor, Perkins had a relationship with seven parishes in six dioceses over the course of her life: The Church of the Holy

Spirit, Lake Forest, Illinois, in the Diocese of Chicago; St. Clement's, Philadelphia, in the Diocese of Pennsylvania; Grace Church, Manhattan, and the Church of the Resurrection, Manhattan, both in the Diocese of New York; St. James, Capitol Hill, in the Diocese of Washington; St. Andrew's, Newcastle, in the Diocese of Maine; and St. John's, Ithaca, in the Diocese of Central New York.

This book draws heavily on the St. Bede Lectures which Perkins delivered at St. Thomas' Church, Fifth Avenue, in the winter of 1948, and from extensive research in her private papers at Columbia University, Radcliffe College, and Cornell University. Additional research included the Maurice Reckitt Papers at the University of Sussex, the archives of the Diocese of New York and the General Theological Seminary, and the extensive collection of Anglo-Catholic material at St. Deiniol's-Gladstone's Library in Hawarden, Wales; Pusey House and the Bodleian Libraries in Oxford; and the Lambeth Palace Library. Personal interviews with clergy who knew Perkins, surviving colleagues, students, and members of her family have also informed this work.

Special thanks are due to Tomlin Perkins Coggeshall, grandson of Frances Perkins and founder of the Frances Perkins Center in Newcastle, Maine, for his support of this work. I am also indebted to his mother, the late Susanna Coggeshall, who first granted me permission to use the St. Bede Lectures with the suggestion that they should be published.

The life of the independent scholar has infinite rewards, but institutional and financial support is not one of them. In addition to the many friends who have provided emotional and financial support over the years, I want to acknowledge the support of those rare bodies willing to invest in the work of unaffiliated scholars: the Stewart Lawton Fellowship for Studies in the Liberal Catholic Tradition in Anglicanism at St. Deiniol's/Gladstone's Library; the Historical Society of the Episcopal Church; the Episcopal Women's History Project; the Frances Perkins Center and St. Andrew's, Newcastle; the Economic Justice Committee of the Diocese of New York; The Church of St. Monica and St. James, Washington, DC; Community Church of New York; the Princeton Research Forum; and all those benefactors who made my education at the General Theological Seminary possible.

And finally, I am indebted to my research assistants: Millicent Browne, my General Seminary colleague, who among other tasks provided invaluable assistance transcribing materials written in Perkins' own hand, and Matthew Frederick Neumann, my student at Princeton Theological Seminary, who undertook a variety of research tasks and read the penultimate draft of the manuscript.

The Divine Architect
used this soul mightily. Frances
Perkins was a sensitive instrument
in His hands. She listened, she heard,
and she executed.

—Mother Catherine Grace
All Saints Sisters of the Poor

Chapter One

A Story of Vocation

It was a rainy Sunday in March of 1934. Silver vases filled with pink roses, white snapdragons, blue iris, and lilies of the valley graced the President's dinner table. The latter, symbols of humility in Christian art, are also associated with the human ability to envision a better world. Whether anyone knew of the symbolism or not, the flowers surely provided welcome relief to the guests who had endured not just a day of gloom but a full year of crisis and criticism.

The occasion was the first anniversary of the inauguration of Franklin Delano Roosevelt as President of the United States. The principals of the fledgling administration had just returned from Mt. St. Alban, the highest point in the District of Columbia, where they had joined the President and First Lady at a special anniversary service at Washington Cathedral.

Now seated around the dinner table, the inner circle of the New Deal formed a tableau of life as Episcopalians would have it be: reverent, chastened, responsible, hopeful.

Newspaper accounts noted that Frances Perkins attended the dinner unescorted.[1] Although she was indeed someone's wife and someone else's mother, she was not there for either of those reasons, nor was she there because she was a close friend of the President, although that description was true as well. She was there because she was a part of that inner circle, a key player on the New Deal team, the first woman ever to serve in a Presidential cabinet.

What led to her presence at table that day?

Both contemporary witnesses and latter-day observers would probably recite the complex set of historical circumstances that propelled her into that moment. But Perkins herself would have stated unequivocally that it was none other than Jesus Christ. She had responded to a call, and this was where her vocation had led.

By the time she stepped down as Secretary of Labor in 1945, she would have provided countless American workers with protection against unemployment and workplace injury. She would have ushered in the eight-hour day and the 40-hour workweek, with provision for overtime pay for hourly workers. She would have provided virtually all the country's children with protection against the loss of a wage-earning parent. And she would have lifted millions of elderly Americans out of poverty. All of these miracles were achieved through her design, development, and advocacy of a social insurance system larger than anything previously attempted anywhere in the world. But all these achievements came after she had attained the age of fifty-two. They were preceded by thirty years devoted to works of mercy in the "haunts of wretchedness and need" invoked by Frank Mason North in a hymn which asks Jesus to "tread the city's streets again."[2] And they were followed by another ten years of teaching in the School of Industrial and Labor Relations at Cornell University.

Despite the unprecedented level of national leadership she attained, Perkins saw herself as a *follower* of Christ rather than a *leader* of church or society. In a letter written in the autumn of 1944 to priest, author, and long-time personal friend, Bernard Iddings Bell, she said "when it comes to the church, I have always been a learner, and certainly on every count I can think of I ought to remain in that role for a long time."[3]

Without attempting to second guess the wisdom of her judgment, it seems fitting to suggest that a half century after her death, the time has come for the church to learn from Frances Perkins. No better summary of her ministry (a word chosen advisedly) and self-understanding can be found than her contribution to the St. Bede Lectures at Manhattan's St. Thomas Church, Fifth Avenue, in 1948, which will be the topics of Chapters Two, Three, and Four.

In these three chapters, Frances Perkins, mostly in her own words, will reveal the theological understanding that inspired and sustained her long career as an architect of the modern city of God.

* * *

Born in 1880, Fannie Coralie Perkins was of solid Yankee stock, baptized at the age of seven in the Plymouth Congregational Church in Worcester, Massachusetts. Yet it seems this humanistic, iconoclastic tradition had limited capacity to speak to a young girl with a passion for the visual arts and a zest for nature. First the daughter and later the mother of professional artists, and eventually the grandmother of an environmentalist, she herself sketched. She published articles on historic preservation and was an avid museum-goer. And she majored in the natural sciences at Mt. Holyoke. She graduated in 1902 as president of her class.

As a college student, Perkins had several experiences that crystallized her sense of vocation. She was deeply influenced by the now-classic photo essay, *How the Other Half Lives* by Jacob Riis. (Although it is unlikely that she knew it at the time, Riis himself was an active Episcopalian, who would later serve on the church's national Commission on the Relations of Capital and Labor.) A campus lecture by the dynamic Florence Kelley of the National Consumers League planted the idea that the individual can make a difference. And then a course with Professor Annah May Soule gave her concrete experience in the field of social work. Perkins and her classmates were sent into the factories of Holyoke to make surveys of working conditions. George Martin, in his 1978 biography of Perkins, said the course gave her "the opportunity to use her scientific training to test and build conclusions in a humanistic field. She discovered that one serious injury—say, the loss of a man's hand—could drive a steady, sober working family into penury. Factory work, she learned, was so irregular that savings were continually exhausted. Avoiding poverty therefore was not a question of simply liquor or laziness but also of safety devices on machines and of regularity of employment."[4]

Is it any wonder Perkins lost patience with those religious perspectives that emphasized personal responsibility and moral improvement when the problems she saw were so often mechanical or systemic? Her enthusiasm for the laboratory and the field investigation may also have fostered a desire for the more experiential approach to truth found in liturgical traditions rich in art, drama, and nature imagery.

She had already decided that she would go into social work upon graduation, but she was rebuffed in her initial attempts to enter the field. (There were no degrees for it in those days.) Necessity required her to take a series of teaching jobs, the last being at Ferry Hall in staunchly Presbyterian Lake Forest, Illinois. She hated the job, partly because it was not what she wanted to do, but possibly also because she found herself unwilling to be a handmaiden of Calvinist pedagogy.

She addressed the first part of this dilemma by working weekends in settlement houses, first at the Chicago Commons, which focused on industrial issues and union organizing, and then at Hull House, the famous settlement founded by Jane Addams and her friend, Ellen Gates Starr.

Embracing Anglo-Catholicism and the Episcopal Church

In the spring of 1905, Perkins presented herself for confirmation at the Church of the Holy Spirit, then a fledgling Anglo-Catholic beacon in Lake Forest, effectively resolving the second part of her dilemma.

Catholic tradition understands confirmation as a sacramental rite in which Christians "confirm" the vows which they made (or which their sponsors made on their behalf) in baptism. Widely understood as a "coming of age" ritual, it became a custom in some parts of Western Christianity to take a new name, signifying that the confirmand was now taking charge of his or her life.[5] Following this ancient practice, Perkins took a new name at confirmation and would henceforth be known to the world as *Frances* Perkins.

Little is known about what led Perkins to embrace Anglo-Catholicism. It was much more than a mere change of denominations. George Martin in his 1976 biography, *Madam*

The blossoming of the ecumenical movement in the years since the second Vatican Council (1962-1965) have blurred many of the distinctions that characterized Roman Catholicism and the various Protestant communions since the Council of Trent (1545-1563) launched the Counter-Reformation. While exceptions certainly existed, this chart contrasts historic differences.

Catholic	Protestant
The God of Grace	The God of Judgment
Divine Initiative	Human Liberty
Providence	Prudence
Affirmative	Critical
Stable	Dynamic
Pastoral	Prophetic
Relationships	Principles
Inherited relationships	Intentional relationships
Sensory	Cerebral
Visual	Auditory
Sin as failure	Sin as rebellion
Forgiveness	Accountability
Humanity essentially good	Humanity totally depraved
Accommodation	Challenge
Realist (Aristotelian)	Idealist (Platonic)
Concrete	Abstract
Body	Spirit
God as immanent	God as transcendent
Cyclical	Linear
Existential	Eschatological
Authority of Nature	Human Dominion over Nature
Systemic	Personal
Values the past	Rejects the past
Future continues the past	Future is radically new
Authority of Tradition	Authority of Scripture
Gospel of John	Epistles of Paul

Secretary, noted that at one point Perkins had told her parents she was considering a conversion to Roman Catholicism.

"Almost nothing could have upset them more," he wrote. To a Congregational family in New England at the beginning of the twentieth century, "it was just conceivable that in Baltimore or New Orleans an educated person might be Catholic; in New England, with only the rarest exceptions, it was not."[6]

Their view was not uncommon for its time. Many Americans saw the authoritarianism associated with Roman Catholicism as a threat to democracy. Its association with working class immigrants and its support of the trade union movement also threatened the business class.

It is possible that Perkins' Hull House connections may have opened up another possibility. Co-founder Ellen Gates Starr was a practicing Anglo-Catholic. It might have been Starr who encouraged Perkins to explore this less-threatening Anglican alternative to papal Catholicism.

While spending her weekends at Hull House, Perkins would have had ample opportunity to immerse herself in the varieties of catholic worship in the city's many parishes. The Episcopal Diocese of Chicago has historically been a "catholic" diocese, part of a regional grouping known as the "Biretta Belt"— playfully named for the distinctive liturgical headdress worn only by the most catholic-minded Episcopal clergy at that time. If Starr had indeed been a party to this quest, she no doubt would have provided answers to many of Perkins' questions and provided introductions to others making similar explorations.

In her 2009 biography, *The Woman Behind the New Deal*, Kirstin Downey speculated that social advantage might have been part of Perkins' motivation. She noted that members of the Armour and Swift families (meat-packing) and the Morton (salt) family had been part of a fund-raising event for Holy Spirit only a week after Perkins was confirmed.[7] However, George Martin saw it differently.

"Evidently there was no thought of social advantage in her conversion;" he wrote. The social pedigree of the Congregational Church (now part of the United Church of Christ) outranked the Episcopal Church in both Maine and Massachusetts. "As for Lake Forest," he noted, "the swells were Presbyterians; the local story is that the Presbyterians helped to build the Episcopal church in order to provide their Church of England butlers with a place to worship."[8]

Historically, there has been very little theological difference between Congregationalism and Presbyterianism. Both rightly claim to be standard bearers of Reformed (Calvinistic) Protestantism. The difference mainly concerns polity. In the Congregational Church, authority is vested in the local church body. In the Presbyterian Church, authority is vested in a hierarchy of elected councils—session, presbytery, synod, and general assembly.

An embrace of Anglo-Catholicism, then, represented a significant departure from Perkins' own heritage as well as the dominant patterns of mainline Protestantism. It was something completely different and, in the eyes of many Reformed Protestants, a throwback to the "Dark Ages."

In some respects, this criticism was accurate. Anglo-Catholicism grew out of the Oxford Movement in England, a conservative reaction to the liberalization of Parliament, which had been opened to Protestant Dissenters from the Establishment in 1828 and to Roman Catholics in 1829. This liberalization meant that people who were not members of the Church of England had governing authority over it.

In 1833 John Keble climbed into the pulpit at Oxford's University Church of St. Mary the Virgin to preach a sermon entitled *National Apostasy*. The sermon assailed a recent Parliamentary decision to reduce the number of bishops in Ireland by almost half, suggesting that Parliament was beginning to treat the church as if it were just another department of the state. The ancient understanding of the bishops as successors to the Apostles commissioned by Christ himself had to be reasserted, Keble argued.

This assertion resonated deeply with the vicar of St. Mary the Virgin, John Henry Newman and his Oxford colleagues, such as Richard Hurrell Froude, Edward Bouverie Pusey, and others who began writing a series of publications known as *Tracts for the Times.*

What started in Oxford soon became an international movement within the Anglican Communion. By 1847, the founders of St. Mark's Church in Philadelphia would state in the parish charter that they sought to advance the principles of the Oxford Movement. Like their counterparts around the world, they would emphasize the historic catholic nature of Anglicanism—comprehensive, sacramental, incarnational, and stable—in contrast to the individualist, intellectual, transcendent, and dynamic emphases of Reformed and Evangelical Protestantism. Divine initiative and an affirmative, compassionate view of human nature contrasted with Protestantism's emphasis on human liberty and its critical, some would say negative, view of human nature.

While the sermon that touched off the Oxford Movement[9] concerned the changing relationship of church and state in England, subsequent generations of theologians and ethicists sought to bring this incarnational theology to bear on the social dislocations and injustices of the industrial revolution.

Social Implications of the Sacraments

The year 1889 saw the publication of *Lux Mundi: A Series of Studies in the Religion of the Incarnation*. Edited by the Rev. Charles Gore, who would later become Bishop of Oxford, the book was a collection of twelve essays which sought to reconcile the historic catholic faith with modern developments, such as biblical criticism and science, and translate it into social action.

That same year Gore and many of the contributors to *Lux Mundi* formed the Christian Social Union to study how to apply Christian moral principles to social and economic problems. Within a few years, it had a counterpart in the Episcopal Church in the United States.

By the time of Perkins' conversion, alleviation of poverty and advocacy of a just social order were widely understood to be the logical implications of the sacramental and incarnational worldview of Anglo-Catholicism.

Two years after she joined the church, Perkins received a job offer from the Philadelphia Research and Protective Association, which would be her first paid professional assignment in social work. The association was an interfaith venture incubated by the Diocese of Pennsylvania to address the plight of young immigrant women who were forced into sexual slavery. New arrivals to the city were often met at the trains by men from their ethnic or language group who offered to show them to lodgings.

These boarding houses were essentially bordellos, where the young women were drugged and offered to paying customers.[10]

As executive secretary of the association, Perkins was responsible for training women from those various ethnic groups to meet the trains themselves, warn the unsuspecting arrivals about the scam, and furnish them with legitimate resources.[11]

Through this work Perkins learned that African-American women arriving from the South faced the same problems. While historians cite 1917 as the beginning of the "Great Migration", more than two hundred thousand Southern blacks had already made their way to the industrial cities of the North during the first decade of the twentieth century.[12]

Perkins argued to her board that these African-American women from the rural South, even though they spoke English and were American citizens, were for all intents and purposes immigrants, too. She was successful in persuading her board to allow her to add two African-American women to her staff.

Perkins and her team did more than just meet the trains. It was their responsibility to identify pimps and drug dealers, disreputable boarding houses, and dishonest employment agencies and try to put them out of business. They also had to maintain up-do-date lists of reputable boarding houses and legitimate employment agencies to which new arrivals could be safely referred.

Perkins knew who the pimps and thugs were—some of them by name, and they knew who she was, too. One rainy night about 11 p.m., as Perkins made her way home, she realized she was being followed. Most likely walking west on Walnut Street, she would have eventually turned onto one of the much darker numbered streets. Although Philadelphia had electric street lighting on the main thoroughfares at the time, the lights were extremely bright carbon arc lamps (one to a block and no longer used for public lighting). The numbered streets most likely still had gas lighting and would have appeared extremely dark to anyone turning off the main street.[13]

"The faster she walked, the faster they followed. She recalled her father's advice for such an occasion. Rounding a corner, she stopped, turned, lowered her umbrella so they collided with it and began to scream the name of the man she knew: 'Sam Smith! Sam Smith!' Along the street windows went up, heads came out, and the men fled" according to George Martin.[14]

The police agreed to shut down the men's agency provided that Perkins could deliver her socially prominent board members to City Hall when the owners protested. Eventually, the association obtained passage of a city ordinance requiring all lodgings to be licensed.

Evidence suggests that Perkins worshiped at St. Clement's, another Anglo-Catholic beacon, located at Twentieth and Cherry Streets not too far from the Philadelphia Museum of Art. She may have begun her lifelong relationship with All Saints Sisters of the Poor at that time.[15] The sisters had acquired the small hospital for the poor previously operated by the parish, and they made it their mission base in Philadelphia, carrying on an active ministry in the parish. The building still stands and is now a part of Moore College of Art.

Perkins eventually became an associate of the order. During her twelve years in the New Deal cabinet, she would spend one day a month in silent retreat at the sisters' Catonsville, Maryland, convent. (In 2009, a majority of the sisters at Catonsville were received into the Roman Catholic Church, but it was an Episcopal order throughout the period when Perkins was an associate.)

Although Perkins was in Philadelphia for only two years, she was very busy. She joined the Socialist Party of America and taught classes in sociology and economics at the diocesan headquarters while taking courses at the Wharton School of the University of Pennsylvania under the legendary political economist, Simon Patten, whose influence extended to the fields of sociology and social work.

A life-long Presbyterian, Patten was nonetheless a critic of Calvinism and sought to modify his church's embrace of it. Among other concerns, he believed it lacked an appreciation of nature and placed emphasis on individual salvation at the expense of community.[16] In the economic sphere, he advocated regulation of the economy but was critical of Marxist theory because of its coercive tendencies.

On Patten's recommendation, Perkins went to New York in 1909 to pursue a master's in political science at Columbia University. While there, she resided first at Hartley House, a settlement house on West Forty-Sixth Street, then later at Greenwich House, near Sheridan Square, both of which remain in active service at their original locations.

Greenwich House had been founded by Mary Kingsbury Simkhovitch. Like Perkins, Simkhovitch had been raised a New England Congregationalist but, inspired by the Cowley fathers of the Society of St. John the Evangelist, she had converted to Anglo-Catholicism when she was in college. She was also schooled in socialist thought, having attended the International Socialist Trade Union Congress in 1889. Her husband, Vladimir Simkhovitch, was a professor at Columbia and also a convert to Anglo-Catholicism.

Upon graduation from Columbia, Perkins was hired by the National Consumers League, an organization which organized consumers to press retailers and manufacturers to provide safe working conditions, rest breaks, and adequate pay for their employees. In addition to organizing volunteers to request meetings with management officials, Perkins also served as the League's chief lobbyist in Albany. In this capacity, she was instrumental in obtaining passage of the 54-hour bill, a landmark piece of labor legislation prohibiting women of any age and boys under eighteen from working more than fifty-four hours in a single week.

The Triangle Factory Fire

Then on a fateful Saturday afternoon in 1911, Perkins was having tea with friends near Washington Square when they heard the clamor of horse-drawn fire trucks rushing to the east side of the square. The eighth, ninth, and tenth floors of the Asch Building were ablaze. The floors were home to the Triangle Shirtwaist Company, manufacturers of the famous "Gibson Girl" blouses. Despite eight fires in nine years of operation, the owners had refused to hold fire drills. Successful in their efforts to defeat unionization, the fire exits had been chained shut to keep workers in and organizers out.

Now the Triangle was on fire again—*for the last time*. All told, one hundred forty-six people died and an untold number were injured. Forty-seven women, some with flaming hair and clothing, jumped from the windows. Firemen tried to break their fall with nets and blankets, but the bodies hit with such force that the firemen somersaulted, the horses stampeded, and bodies crashed right through the sidewalks.

"The New Deal was born on March 25, 1911," Perkins would later say.

An outraged citizenry formed the Committee on Safety. With the blessing of the Consumer's League, Perkins accepted an assignment as the executive secretary. The Committee, in turn, "lent" her to the state legislature's newly created Factory Investigating Commission, organized by Al Smith, who would later become governor of New York and, in 1928, the first Roman Catholic ever nominated for President.

In this work, her belief in experiential learning and her preference for liturgy combined. *Preaching* to the legislators about the problem was not enough. She would take these overweight, cigar-chomping pols on surprise visits to factories at five o'clock in the morning, take them over to the window and point to the ice-covered wooden ladder propped against the wall, and say, "There, gentlemen. That's your fire escape." And out the window and down the slippery ladder they went.

The result was that New York State, which accounted for one-third of the Gross National Product at this time, also led the nation in factory safety legislation.

She got away with these exercises, she later said, because she had learned early on that, in her sober manner of dress and her trademark tricorne hat, she reminded these men of their mothers. (These "liturgical" exercises included vestments!) As she put it, "I said to myself, 'That's the way to get things done. So behave, so dress, so comport yourself that you subconsciously remind them of their mothers.'"

Marriage and Motherhood

She would soon become a mother herself. In 1913 she married Paul C. Wilson in the Chantry of Grace Church in Greenwich Village. Three years later, her daughter Susanna was born.

Wilson was the scion of a wealthy Chicago business family who had immersed himself in the good government movement. He had been working for the Bureau of Municipal Affairs when Frances first met him. He subsequently joined the reform administration of John Purroy Mitchel. For both professional and political reasons, the couple made a principled decision that Frances should continue to use the Perkins name. She had already made a national name for herself as a fire safety expert. Separate names for the public advocate and the public official seemed to make sense, although they made no secret of their marriage.

Susanna's birth had been preceded by two unsuccessful pregnancies. The first resulted in a miscarriage. During the second pregnancy, Perkins developed pre-eclampsia, a pregnancy-induced illness that was often fatal. It required Perkins to take to bed and finally to have a cesarean section. The baby, a boy, was stillborn. Following a long illness, Perkins joined with her friends in founding New York's first maternity center to promote healthy pregnancies and well babies. More women and babies died in childbirth in the United States than in any other developed country. With Perkins as the unpaid executive secretary, the program was expanded city-wide and was eventually credited with improving infant survival by twenty-nine percent and reducing maternal deaths by sixty percent.

About eighteen months after Perkins started this work, she gave birth to Susanna Perkins Wilson, who would be her only child and the mother of her only grandchild, Tomlin Perkins Coggeshall, who would become the apple of his grandmother's eye in her senior years.[17]

Within a year of Susanna's birth, Mayor Mitchel was turned out of office in a humiliating defeat. Wilson not only lost his job, but he also lost a substantial portion of his wealth speculating in gold stocks. Work was no longer a matter of choice for Perkins. Within a few years, Wilson had developed a mental illness eventually requiring hospitalization. From that point on, Perkins was the breadwinner for her family.

From Public Interest Advocate to Public Official

When Al Smith was elected governor in 1918, he wanted to appoint Perkins as Industrial Commissioner, the position that preceded the formation of the state Department of Labor. Despite her need for employment, Perkins was reluctant to accept the appointment. She believed her call was to be a public interest *advocate* not a public *official*, but Smith persuaded her that good people had to take responsibility for change. Preaching was not enough. Somebody had to translate the ideal into daily reality. The Word, it could be said, had to become Flesh. Advising her to join the Democratic Party, Smith became her political mentor and the closest thing she ever had to a hero.

While taking on these new responsibilities, Perkins continued to deepen her faith. Steeped more in Thomas Aquinas than in the giants of the Protestant Social Gospel, Perkins was a student of the social encyclicals emanating from the papacy, beginning with *Rerum Novarum* in 1891, which endorsed the trade union movement. During the 1920s, she toured New York state with a Roman Catholic priest in an effort to educate the public about the content of these encyclicals.

She also made several trips to England, partly to study the unemployment insurance system, but also to participate in the

Anglo-Catholic Summer School of Christian Sociology. The Summer School met at Oxford University and published *Christendom*, a high-caliber socialist journal. The summer school was a very sophisticated, invitation-only, educational enterprise that required a 12-week course of preparation. Perkins' fellow students included William Temple, who would later become Archbishop of Canterbury, the economic historian R.H. Tawney, the literary theologians T.S. Eliot and Dorothy Sayers, and a young Joseph Fletcher, destined to make his mark in the field of ethics.[18]

When Roosevelt was elected governor in 1928, Frances Perkins was already prepared to develop workers compensation and unemployment insurance systems for New York state. But she was reluctant to come to Washington when he was elected President in four years later. She had good reason to stay put. Herbert Lehman, the newly elected governor of New York, had asked her to stay on. FDR had not actually committed to social insurance during the campaign. She had a daughter in school and a husband in a sanitarium. She loved her work. She loved New York, and she said in her reminiscences that she adored her little parish church, the Church of the Resurrection in the East Seventies near where she lived.

The American Federation of Labor opposed her appointment because she was not from the ranks of organized labor, but a number of women's groups were actively promoting her appointment. And Charles Gilbert, suffragan bishop of New York, told her he believed it was "God's own call."[19]

And so a deal was struck. If Roosevelt wanted her in the cabinet, he would have to commit to social insurance. He agreed but warned that he knew nothing about it. "You'll have to invent the way to do these things, Frances," he told her. Not to worry. She had already consulted people at IBM to ask if it would be possible to develop a record-keeping system for a population the size of the United States, about one hundred thirty-five million at the time. She learned that it was.

The cause of social insurance was nothing less than a religious quest for Perkins. She believed insurance was the most moral concept humankind had ever developed because it harnessed the generous impulse of neighbor to help neighbor with human technical skill in the form of actuarial science. By applying human intelligence to the best aspect of the human spirit, neighbor could help neighbor even before tragedy struck.

Protecting Her Interior Space

It is overwhelming to consider the magnitude of the challenge she took on, especially considering that she had to be the Secretary of Labor at a time when twenty-five percent of the labor force nationally was out of work. In some locales, it was as high as eighty percent.

Mother Virginia of All Saints Sisters of the Poor grasped the scope of the problem in a reflection on Perkins' time at the convent.

"Her anonymity was carefully guarded by the Sisters who always referred to her as Mrs. Wilson [Mrs. Paul Wilson]. Frances spent many hours in the Convent chapel and was there frequently even during the times when chapel was being swept. Frances Perkins valued her long talks with Mother Laura—a very wise and discreet Religious, in those years of her great and awesome responsibilities. These times were balanced by long walks through the surrounding country with the Assistant Superior, another great friend of Miss Perkins."[20]

Perkins toyed with the idea of living in a convent went she first moved to Washington. Because her family would not be coming with her and because she correctly anticipated how stressful her job would be, the combination of solitude and community appealed to her. However, she also recognized that the press would have a field day with it, and she did not want her religious sensibilities or those of the nuns subjected to ridicule.

From the moment her appointment was announced, there was concern in the press about why she continued to be known as "Miss Perkins" when she had been married for almost twenty years and had a teenaged daughter. Moreover, she had had a difficult relationship with the press from the earliest days of her career. She was impatient, and often showed it, with reporters who would ask questions about decisions that had not yet been made. Way back in her Hull House days, she had learned to dodge reporters who were often looking for evidence of anarchist plots among the settlement house clientele.

Ultimately, she decided to live with friends. The first with Daisy Harriman (Florence Jaffray Harriman), who would go on to found the Women's National Democratic Club. The second was Mary Harriman Rumsey, (Daisy was the widow of Mary's first cousin, Borden). Mary had founded the Junior League and numerous other organizations. And the last was Caroline O'Day, who had been elected congresswoman-at-large for New York state with the help of both Franklin and Eleanor Roosevelt.

All three women were active Episcopalians from the Diocese of New York. All three had worked with Perkins in various shared endeavors from the beginning of her career. All three were wealthy enough to subsidize Perkins, and all three cared deeply about her work.

Daisy Harriman, who eventually became U.S. Envoy to Norway, reflected in her book, *Mission to the North,* on the time Perkins spent at her home.

"My close-up of our Secretary of Labor disclosed a woman with a phenomenal capacity for hard work. 'Horny-handed sons of toil' and kibitzing left-wing journalists often harped on her 'bourgeois origin', and the woman's clubs claimed her as one of themselves who had made good. But the President had known quite well what he was about. No man could possibly have worked harder; nor accepted so simply the physical buffeting of long hours and continuous traveling. Many nights the office discussions of the day would be transferred to my terrace and would go on into the night, midnight, one, two or even three o'clock. I marvelled at the endurance and the patience of the Secretary of Labor who, after the burdens of the day, could graciously give her attention to visitor after visitor who came to consult her on suggested NRA codes. One time, when rather drab discussions were dragging on, a telephone call from the President made her laugh outright. 'You should be happy tonight,' he said, 'I have just signed the code for brassières,'" she wrote.

"On one occasion, Frances had made a speech in New York, and motored all night to get back in time to be at her desk in the morning. She had had interviews all day; and there had been late-staying guests for dinner, all wanting her advice. She went to bed at midnight, but at half past one my telephone rang violently. 'I *must* speak to Miss Perkins,' said a voice from New York. I hated to wake her but Mr. Alexander Sachs would not take no for an answer. For over an hour I heard the steady, patient voice of the Secretary of Labor, explaining, countering, quietly debating. There is no time clock for any cabinet officer but, at times I thought that, for Frances, there was no clock at all."[21]

At the end of her long Washington sojourn, "Frances returned to New York and to the Church of the Resurrection, where the Rev. Charles Owen Moore, fresh out of the General Theological Seminary, became her spiritual director in her last days.

"Frances Perkins was petite, but she radiated a powerful personal presence," he wrote. "She filled my study the moment she came into the room, not with a sense of self-importance but with a clarity of focus, a seriousness of intent, and an engaging humility that challenged me to meet her straight on…. She had great concern and love for her family and friends, about whom we frequently talked. She observed a rule of prayer that formed the foundation for her daily life. She wanted to prepare for her death still living life to the full, aware that she was going to be with the God she already knew and loved."[22]

The historical record shows that she seems to have done just that. She made her last retreat at All Saints convent just three weeks before she died, and she delivered her last lecture at Cornell University just four days before she entered life eternal on May 14, 1965.

Above: The Church of the Holy Spirit, Lake Forest, Illinois, as it looked when Perkins was confirmed there in 1905.

At left: St. Clement's, Philadelphia, where Perkins worshiped from 1907 to 1910. The Cowley Fathers of the Society of St. John the Evangelist operated the parish from 1874 to 1891. The All Saints Sisters of the Poor were in residence during Perkins' tenure.

Chapter Two

A Christian Order of Society

In 1916, the Episcopal Church, meeting in General Convention, adopted a resolution stating that "the service of the community and the welfare of the workers, *not primarily profit* [emphasis added], should be the aim of every industry and its justification; and that the church should seek to keep this aim constantly before the mind of the public…"

With the New York State 54-hour bill already under her belt, the church's statement in 1916 was more a ratification of what Frances Perkins already believed than an idea that gave impetus to her vocation. It is worthy of note here, however, because in the first of her St. Bede presentations, "A Christian Order of Society," she explains what she means by a "Christian" understanding of the purposes of economic activity. And she offers her view of how the church should meet its responsibility to keep these principles in the public mind.

Perkins was one of three presenters, each of whom delivered three weekly lectures. The very subjects chosen by the lecture committee provide some clues about what Episcopalians were thinking in 1948. The first three talks were presented by Father Shirley C. Hughson, a monk from the Order of the Holy Cross. Grouped under the heading of "The Religious Life," Hughson's topics included: "Its Origin, Nature, and Purpose," "Its Effect in the History of the Church and the World," and "The Need of the Spirit in the Religious Life Today."

Perkins presented the second segment, under the heading of "The Christian in the World." Her topics included "A Christian Order of Society," "The Vocation of the Laity," and "The Good Life, Community and Individual." Her series was followed by three sessions on "The Unity of Christendom" by the Rev. Powell Mills Dawley, who was then professor of ecclesiastical history at the General Theological Seminary. Dawley's presentations included "Our Heritage of Disunion," "The Ecumenical Movement," and "Anglican Responsibility and Opportunity."[23]

Sandwiched between two priests, one a monk and the other a seminary professor, Perkins was in impressive company, yet in these lectures, as in most other aspects of her career, she shows herself to be equal to the task.

*   *   *

A group comprised of mostly Episcopalians and mostly New Yorkers gathered in the warm glow of the Guild Hall of St. Thomas Church, Fifth Avenue, on a Monday night in late January of 1948 for the first of Frances Perkins' Bede presentations. Many in the audience knew her personally.

Earlier that week, both the National Women's Trade Union League and the National Council of Jewish Women had urged Congress to extend war-time controls on the price of meat.[24] Fuel rationing seemed imminent as a fuel shortage plagued the nation.

The dawning of the "Atomic Age" was on everyone's mind. The partition of Palestine and the growing consolidation of communist power in Eastern and Central Europe threatened the tenuous peace which followed the most devastating war in recorded history. Before the end of the three-week period in which Perkins delivered these lectures, Pope Pius XII would call for a ban on the atom bomb.

Former Vice President Henry A. Wallace, Perkins' New Deal colleague and a fellow worshipper at St. James, Capitol Hill, her beloved parish in Washington, had announced a third-party candidacy for President, with world peace as a primary focus.

Amid this backdrop, Perkins began her remarks on a note of humor, saying she felt she owed the audience an "explanation, perhaps an apology for being here at all" adding that "it is almost as much of a surprise to me as it must be to you to find me lecturing on so profound a religious subject."[25]

She said she was brought up on the theory that the laity should keep silent.

"I was taught to listen and learn, and I got to be pretty good at it. I was taught certainly it was unthinkable that laywomen should open their mouths with regard to any of these matters." She went on to tease the audience about the wisdom of that teaching.

"Well, I don't know but what I agree that's a good idea," she said, playing into common stereotypes about women. "Well…we can say it between ourselves. So many [laywomen] are here. Our besetting sin is politically called discursiveness, which means talking too much, you know; and the other one crowding close upon it is, well, domination, which is an aspect of pride, I believe, but in the family known as bossiness."

Facetiously describing her invitation to speak as a "dangerous experiment" for the St. Bede's Library Lecture Committee, she said that, in addition to a very persuasive committee, she also felt the weighty words of her pastor.

"My pastor is a disciplinarian of a kind and does not hesitate to point out to his parishioners, whose souls are in his care, where he thinks they are making a mistake. I may say that he wrote me a letter once with regard to my having turned down, with what I thought a good deal of style, an invitation to speak on some religious subject, saying that that wasn't my line." Noting that she referred them to the bishop, she said her rector, the Rev. [Gordon] Wadhams told her that "the laity must bear witness at some time in their lives, and that they must offer what they have. And if it isn't very good, that's the best they can do. They must offer what they have and what their life experience has brought them, and what little their training and education may have developed" in them an understanding of the principles "lying back of the religious life" and the religious and moral duties laypeople undertake.

"So, here I am" she continued, "to discuss these matters as best I can and to say to you that I have long thought about this subject of what the Christian in the world ought to do and can do and has a responsibility to do." She said for years she had observed Christians of her generation trying to "Christianize" the world. "I think that much of the effort, which we have observed in the first half of this century toward the building up of…a better social order, has been an honestly conceived…effort to Christianize the world, to make it better, to make it, at least so far as our country and our state and our city are concerned, a place fit for Christians to live in, a place fit for human beings to grow up in and to bring up their families in, and train their children in."

Noting that while the topic seemed modest enough, it had nonetheless generated a sizable literature. "And when I looked over the shelf of books of which even St. Bede's Library has that bear upon this subject, I realize that this matter has entertained the great doctors and scholars of the world for many years, and that the amount of literature on this subject is enormous.

"The only comfort I have in discussing the matter with you is that I am quite sure that only a few of you have ever read any of the literature on the subject," she teased, drawing laughter from the audience.

"However, spurred on by one member of the committee, I made a bibliography....It is not a real bibliography because it is by no means inclusive, and I haven't annotated it. And I haven't quoted from those books at all. They are just interesting books that I saw on the shelf, you know, bearing on this subject. Some of them I have read a little about. Anyhow, I have called it 'Suggested Reading', but it is a whole page of densely type-written material. And that doesn't begin to go into the ancient Fathers who wrote at great length upon the subject of the world and how the Christian should organize his world around him."

Lay Vocation as Responsibility for the Affairs of the World

It is at this point that she zeroed in on what would be the recurring theme of all three lectures, saying, "I suppose if the laity are to talk at all on the subjects of religion, that certainly the subject of 'The Christian in the World' is appropriate, for the worldly matters and world affairs are certainly in these days committed into the hands of the laity. It is the laity that conduct the secular life of the community...and it is the laity, therefore, who must take responsibility for the way these matters are conducted....[for] details and for the principles of how the world's affairs are conducted. And it is the church which must teach them the principles they must apply."

Characteristic of educated speakers of her day, Perkins often used the words "man" and "men" in a generic sense to mean all of humanity as she does in this passage.

"The vocation of the laity, I think, is a vocation to handle the secular affairs as Christians and as *instructed* Christians who know what the end purpose of Man's life on earth is..." So instructed, they can "develop an order and a system in their particular field of operations, which is a Christian system.

"This, I fear, has not been done in the past. I see so many well-intentioned people operating in the government of the United States, we'll say, as I have seen them more recently, who have the vaguest notion of what the end purpose of Man is, and why—if any reason—they are administering a program, we'll say, of Social Security. If you ask most of them closely, they will tell you, 'Well, you know, people need to be taken care of.' In other words, they give you a purely humanitarian answer." For

Perkins, humanitarianism alone was not enough to sustain a lifetime of "Christianizing" the world. She related a story from her days at Hull House, the Chicago settlement.

"I'm often reminded of an episode which I observed when I was quite young and living at Hull House and just moving into the field of social responsibility. There were two young men who both were residents at Hull House, and they were very different types but extremely good social workers, extremely good settlement workers. And we had many discussions…One was a materialist and a humanitarian. The other was a Christian, and I think he called himself a Christian sociologist. He was a very sincere and devout person.

"One day we were going somewhere very early in the morning. I know that it was a snowy day, and hardly anyone was out. The streetcars weren't moving on Halstead Street, and we waited a long time hoping to get a car. Across the street there was a man, a very unkempt and ragged and badly dressed man, whose shoes were all broken. His toes were coming out of the uppers of the shoes, and it was obvious that they were falling to pieces.

"Somebody remarked, 'That man needs a new pair of shoes badly. Is there any way to get him any?' While we discussed that element, I suddenly said to myself, 'I wonder why you want to give him a pair of shoes!'

"As we discussed the matter among us we agreed that this was it: Alan would give him a pair of shoes because his feet were cold and that Bob would give him a pair of shoes for Jesus' sake.

"It was interesting to me because we laughed at it at the moment. The end result would be the same. The man would get the shoes. But today—I have known these men all my life ever since that time—one of them, Alan, is a rich stock broker. He loved social work, but the humanitarian drive just wasn't enough. You know, the poor aren't grateful in the long run, and quarrels come up, and it wasn't easy."

Robert, she noted, was at the head of a great charitable organization in one of the great industrial cities of America. She said, "he still plods on doing that service for human beings, which he does not for humanitarian reasons, but which he does for divine reasons because he understands the end and destiny of the people with whom he is working, and because he understands for himself the obligation to love his fellow man, and has the capacity to love his fellow man within the love of God."

Love Makes a Difference

She said she believed this love of fellow within the love of God "makes a difference in the attitude with which Christians go at a piece of work which is definitely for the welfare of society and for the ordering of our outer life. It makes a difference in the way Christians go at it if they are conscious and instructed

Christians...So, I plead...for a consistent instruction by the clergy and the church to the laity in what the nature of their responsibility is—what the Christian principles are that are to be applied in conducting a bank, in running a business, in operating a labor union, in keeping house and doing the marketing—in any of the multiple activities of the secular life which fall to the lot of Christians. They must be instructed in the principles which they must apply as they make their decisions."

She said that while the world often found itself in a state of confusion, there was, in 1948, a widespread feeling once expressed in a hymn:

> The world is very evil
>
> The times are waxing late,
>
> Be sober and keep vigil,
>
> The king [sic] is at the gate.[26]

"Twenty years ago [i.e., the late 1920s], you could hardly have said that, even in a church community. You wouldn't have been seriously regarded. It would have been thought—well, it is something you sing in church at appropriate times when one is thinking of the Judgment Day. There isn't any question but that he will agree with you. He will nod his head, and he'll take part, as a matter of fact, in endorsing or sponsoring that set of ideas.

"We have been through a lot, of course, in this generation, this first half of the twentieth century. Just look at what's happened! Two world wars, man-made floods and dust storms—not in Central Asia where we knew they'd be reckless with the use of the soil and the resources of nature which God gave them—but man-made floods and dust storms right here in this great country."

Her list continued: "One terrible major economic catastrophe, a near collapse of our economy, which was alarming to the whole of society; two minor ones, not so long or so intense, but of the same nature, and having the same alarming characteristics in that no one knew what to do to counteract the effects of a disturbed economy.

"We have had a deterioration which the man in the street will know and point out to you, a deterioration in public morality to a point where crime prevention, especially for young children and adolescents, is a desperate need; when young people, almost children, are committing crimes so vicious and terrible that the whole community is running around to say how can these be prevented.

"Then we have seen in this first half of the twentieth century a decline of education, oh yes, a great decline in education. More trees but less fruit. More places of education, but less of the fruits of education showing up in our population. Everybody has begun to realize it. Even the taxicab man will tell you that, if you ask him. We have seen a deterioration, a decline, in the quality of our culture which alarms all of us who look around the world and the society in which we live. We have seen a deterioration of the family as an institution for the nurture of the young, and for the organizing and maintaining of man's right social life—not only in divorce—but neglect and failure to establish and to find shelter—shelter in which Christian homes can suitable be built and conducted. This is all a very alarming and frightening picture to those who look at the world as it is.

"Then we have seen the advent of something quite new in Man's make-up and mentality: an incompetence, apparently, an incompetence and incapacity to make peace even when he wants peace and needs peace. [It is] an incapacity with regard to that operation of human relations in which, in older generations at least, they could make peace when they were tired of fighting. Although thy may have had no high-flown notions of what peace was, they were able to achieve a peace, a truce when it was needed and wanted.

"Then we have seen the rise of materialism as a culture, a faith even. And by 'faith' I mean something that people believe it sufficiently so that they take action on it. That's a faith. They act as though it were true. They act on that assumption, on that premise. We have seen the rise of materialism so that thousands, if not the majority of our people, act as though materialism were true and as though it were the real explanation of the world and of the real life in which they find themselves."

Noting that the world had also seen a great expansion in the technical capacities of the human race, she observed that it was accompanied by a decline in the capacity for moral analysis and moral judgment.

"Then we have seen the shrinking, the shriveling of economic man. Quite recently I was noticing this and since it affects us of the comfortable middle classes most of all, we are shrieking about it. We have observed and are experiencing the shrinking of economic man under the economic pressures and phenomena of inflated prices, taxes, and money perversions— money misuses which makes money into a form of power and not a medium of exchange." The result, she said, was that people were feeling "a tremendous sense of loss, of confusion, and of lack of direction" in society.

"Now, the man on the street knows all this. He has observed it. He is profoundly disturbed. Whether he ever goes into a church or not, he is disturbed by our world, and he's frightened. You don't even need to go into melodrama and hiss atoms at him to have him agree with you that the world is very evil. The atom problem has been just one more mystery of disaster added to what he sees has already been a world growing very evil, and the time very late.

"So, he'll join with you in singing, 'Be sober and keep vigil', whether he knows it or not. After all, we have come to the point where we realize that all through the world—How many times have you read it in newspaper articles, in magazine articles, or heard it in offhand speeches here and there, heard someone say—they even say it in high school debating societies—'We have come to the end of an era'? Nobody knows what era or what the one ahead of it is, but it is the fashion to say, 'We have come the end of an era.'"

Technological but not Moral Growth

In emphasizing her point about technological, but not moral growth, she shared a quote she had written down from José Ortega y Gassett's *The Revolt of the Masses*, which she had read a few years earlier. (The book was on the reading list for one of the Summer Schools in the early 1930s.)

"I was impressed by it then. I'm more impressed by it now. Ortega said something like this: "Man. There never was a time when Man believed himself so fabulously capable of creation but does not know what to create.'"

The "scientific penetration of the secrets of the universe" was so enormous, she said, that almost nothing was denied to the human race, yet it did not know what it ought to do.

Some of those who worked on fission of the atom, she noted, have said "if they had even imagined what it would lead to, they would have gone right back to the old farm in Kansas and never gone near a laboratory again...they would not have dared to penetrate. They would not have dared to be creative, if they had known...what they were likely to be bringing into the world's life."

At this point, Perkins introduces what will be her central theological point.

"So, it's a sorry world and a very sobering one in this first half of the twentieth century. I think all of us must be oppressed and depressed by the general climate of despair which is around us with regard to the matters of Man's life on this planet. We have to remember, and we Christians must constantly remind ourselves that in this world, in this generation, there is also our Lord, living and operating through the Incarnation, extended in every part of time and space, operating for the salvation and redemption...of the life of human beings upon this planet."

She said Christians need to remind themselves of that fact. "We think about this thing, that God came and took human form in order that he might redeem human affairs, that he might redeem the pains and sufferings and confusions that men suffer in their life, in their human life, in their natural life upon this planet and that the plan of God was to redeem human nature and to redeem human affairs.

"So, we have God operating—we have the Incarnation operating—also in this half century of despair, this half century which looks to us so terrible and so depressing and so full of questions. We begin to wonder how we can apprehend and appreciate and appropriate and put into the secular activities of human affairs all the truths that are inherent in the truth of the Incarnation extended until this day and upon this place and upon our earth.

"Now, it would be, of course, a mistake to claim that all these things that look so unfortunate are worthy of a near despair. They are discouraging but they are the matters in which the redeeming power of God Incarnate is operating, and in which he asks the loving cooperation of those who know his personal salvation, and who have learned to love him.

"So, the principle of love operating through the universe—if those who know that love will but cooperate—will make even to their limited minds the common sense, the sense of progress which is so necessary for the firm stand, the firm defense of Christian principles as applied to our outward and secular life.

She said Christians must never despair no matter how bad things look. Having been redeemed, they inevitably cannot "stop and say, 'Oh, well, let the old world go. What can I do about that?' That's not possible to us. It is an aspect of our nature and of our redemption that we should continually go on in our effort to assist and cooperate in the establishment of that order of society which seems to us to have been intended by God..."

Saying that it is a question of having to go on, she related a story about the Coast Guard. "In the midst of a terrific storm off the New England coast, one of those really bad ones that comes up around Point Judith, the Coast Guard got a signal of a ship in distress. It had been a long time since they been out because there hadn't been storms that year.

"The young ensign who was to assist in the operation went down to get the boat ready that they might go out, made the readings, read the thermometer, the barometer, the wind pressure, and came rushing back upstairs to the captain and said, 'Captain, we can't go out. It is impossible. We can't go out....The waves are rising. The barometer is falling. It is just impossible. We can't go out.' And the captain, pulling on his great boots, said to him, 'That's all right, boy. We have to go out. We don't have to come back.'

"Coast Guard principles of having to go anyhow—no matter how preposterous or discouraging the situations—are the types of principles and habits that Christians have to apply to themselves when the world looks a little difficult, as it does at the present time. But I want to remind you also...that in this first half of the twentieth century some other things have been happening, too."

Social Progress in the Early Twentieth Century

"In this first half of the twentieth century, we have seen striking and successful developments in the area of Christian action, in the field of social justice. Now, this is really extraordinary that Christian social action practically began with the beginning of this century. It began when the accumulated wealth had come to the point where we noticed surplus. It began when the continent had been conquered; when railroads penetrated from the East to the West; when transportation and communications had been developed to what was then a peak."

She said, within a generation or so it had become apparent that the accumulated wealth exceeded what was needed to sustain families who had made contributions to the development of the economy or to provide new capital for projects yet to be undertaken. Despite what she called some "very silly people" who merely used this surplus wealth, most of the people who had accumulated this sudden wealth "began to think in terms of an obligation to society, of at least a moral relationship to the needs of the community.

"This was before the days of scientific charity, but it was the beginnings really of the laying out of large sums of money for the relief of poverty, for the relief of illness, for the care of the young, and for the development through education of better opportunities.

"We have seen these things happen. We have seen tenement house laws passed right here in New York to get rid of the vermin-ridden, decayed, horrible old tenements. When we say housing legislation today, we mean public appropriations to make possible some brand-new chromium and glass housing somewhere. When we said housing legislation at the beginning of this century, what we really meant" was legislation that would prevent any further development of what were called "old law tenements, which were fire traps, which were dens of disease…, and which were not suitable places for human beings."

She said that tenement house laws were an obvious reform, it nonetheless "cut into the accumulated wealth of the community" and was painful for some people. Next came widow's pensions and then baby clinics.

"Well baby clinics hadn't been heard of in the early years of this century. Babies were sick from drinking bad milk, and so we had baby clinics and public health milk stations…"

Minimum wage and child labor laws followed, she noted, as the public gained awareness of exploitation. People were being asked to work long hours for pay that was too low to support themselves.

"I have always thought it was an interesting thing and, perhaps, a very American way of handling the thing, that accustomed as we are to the town meeting technique of knowing all about everything and doing it by a vote of the meeting, that we turned very naturally to the idea of passing a law when we found that there was exploitation, when we found that people were getting too low wages to buy healthful food. We in America thought without protest in terms of a law.

"But much more than law has happened today, and no only have we gone on with this general legislation all over the country for the improvement of social conditions, but we have in recent years developed a whole scheme of the social insurances to protect individuals against the more acute adversities that may happen to any member of society.

"All this has been a part of a gradually dawning conception that the community, through its organized government, can effect many changes in the aspects of society which are socially undesirable and socially unhealthy.

"In addition to that, we have come to a point where by custom, we'll say—by the habits of the community—factories are not conducted as they used to be conducted. You can hardly find—I suppose I could if I dug for it—some terrible old factories in the City of New York where things look the way practically all factories looked, we'll say, in 1915. But it would be a hard thing to find them because by common consent they have just passed out of the picture, and the modern factory is clean and efficient.

"I often tell the story of one candy factory I knew which was a fire trap, dirty, unsanitary, no machines guarded, the floors covered with chocolate and dirt and sugar all mixed up." She said the young women who worked there were also dirty. "And a few years later, going back and going through the same street, recognizing this factory and remembering the name…I went in. Only one little law had been passed at that time, but the individual who owned and operated the factory—taking advantage of the physical changes he had to make in the property because of the law—had cleaned the whole place up. You had not only two properly protected means of exit, you had all the machinery rearranged—new machinery with the machine guards built in so girls couldn't get their hands cut off. You had caps provided and clean aprons provided for the girls who were making the candy. You had the floor scrubbed. You had none of that filth and disorder which had been characteristic of the factory life at that earlier period.

She said she believed such changes were not from an awakening of public conscience but rather "an extension of human knowledge of how things can be done in decency and order." Nonetheless, she said throughout the movement toward social legislation, Christian points of view were always at work and that the influence of Christians had been great.

She said she remembered with great gratitude the courageous positions of Father Huntington (founder of the Order of the Holy Cross) "when these ideas were new in society and it was debatable whether it was a good idea to pass laws to abolish child labor or to limit the hours of labor of women.

"We shall also be grateful for a clergyman down at the lower end of Fifth Avenue, Percy Grant of the Church of the Ascension, who never was afraid. Now, I never knew why he wasn't afraid of his budget (or anything else) because budgets used to be seriously affected sometimes in those days if a clergyman felt that it was his duty to stand up and go with the committee before the legislature" to testify about what they had seen of human need and how legislative action might correct it."

The Rev. Percy Stickney Grant had been rector of the Church of the Ascension from 1893 through 1924. Perkins knew him well, and they were involved in many of the same activities during the years Perkins lived at Greenwich House and later on Waverly Place. When she and Wilson married, they lived on Washington Place.

Strong Christian Leadership

"We had a great deal of strong Christian leadership in the field of improving our social legislation. Now, churches always taught us, and we always have had a chance to know, what I think has been overlooked during the period of great prosperity in this country…[The church] has taught us about the nature of Man, and has taught us about the nature of Man's relationship to God, and about Man's relationship to other men. That, of course, is the very heart of the social problem, and the problem of creating a Christian social order. The church has taught us that Man is a creature made by God; is an expression of the creative principle that God loved him, and that as an act of creative love, Man, in all of his activities, all of his attributes, all of his powers, has emerged from that creative love…" She said God loves the entire human race as well as individual humans and that God has endowed them with the power to love God.

Because of the power to love God and to love those things which God loves, she said, we understand that the center of the universe is God, and that because we have been given the ability to love the things God loves, we "can be within that creative circle of love" in our attitude toward our fellows. She said the infinite value and worth of the person is not intrinsic. It is value that God has bestowed through love.

"That is a dogma which all are bound to respect in their personal lives and in their social lives. Man is worth everything. He was worth the death on the Cross. He is so infinitely valuable. Even in degradation his value to God is great and must be respected by those who, loving God, love those things which God loves…" She said God loves the degraded and sinful person and we all must do likewise.

"The church has always taught us this, but the church has not perhaps always underscored it so that we who had to handle the affairs of the world and had to deal with" the rights, opportunities, and training and education of others "have always known that. God has taught us, and the church has taught us, that the destiny and end of Man is to know, love, and serve God, and finally, to be joined with him in eternity." Knowing that we are taken up into God's love and that such is the destiny and the end of all humankind, she said, "it's bound to have a modifying effect upon our behavior, upon our decisions as to what we will do with our opportunities to serve men, and particularly with regard to our decisions as to what will really serve men. For there comes a point when the mere handing to men all kinds of things on a platter does not, in any way, truly serve the true nature and destiny of Man. For unless he participates also in this program of building a social order, he does not fulfill his true nature, and he does not make that progress toward God which he is entitled to make."

She said the futility of most of modern conceptions of human destiny could be seen simply by asking the proverbial man-on-the-street.

"What does he think the aims of Man are? Well, financial perhaps. To get rich. That perhaps would be the commonest answer for most people around New York where materialism has made such inroads upon our culture and our thinking." Or someone who was a little more thoughtful "might say, 'Well, the end of Man is to be educated. To get educated. And education will redeem him.' You know how many people in America believe that education will redeem and save men. You put a problem up to a group, to a committee, some official committee that have a responsibility. 'Now, what can we do about this? Here's this very serious problem. What can we do about it?' They all look at each other with long faces, and then someone says, 'The only answer to that is education!' And everybody nods his head and says, 'Yes, education!' It is utter nonsense. Education as we all know it, if we look truthfully at the situation, education as such does not do that." She described education as a "useful tool," but denied its redemptive capacities.

Another concept of destiny "a serious and sober' person will suggest is good citizenship.

"That's a fine aim in life. Good for what? And citizen of what? How does a man know whether he is being a good citizen or not?...Ah, but if he knows, and if the church has taught him, that the law of God is the dominant law, and that it must have precedence and dominance over every law of man, and that the law of Man must be interpreted in the light of the laws of God, then perhaps he can make some headway in being a good citizen.

"I learned a great lesson a good many years ago from an old bureaucrat—just exactly what you call a bureaucrat. He had been in the government service ever since he was eighteen, and he had gone on from one post to another, promoted and promoted and promoted. And as he grew older, he came into higher and higher levels of the Civil Service administration. When I met him, he was at the top of a very important Civil Service function. He was the head of the Civil Service operation of the...Immigration Service of this country.

"Well, I met him almost immediately when I became his superior officer. There came into my office in a few weeks a distressing case of a women who was about to be deported. She was already on Ellis Island before anyone who knew her story got organized enough to communicate with me, and to ask if I couldn't do something about it.

"The woman was deportable all right. She had entered the country illegally a number of years earlier. She came across the border from Canada because she wanted to join the young man she was engaged to. So, she came across the border. She belonged to a country that didn't have a quota at the time. She lived peacefully enough in the place where her husband resided, and she had three small children. She was caught up with by the

Immigration Service through the tattle-tale—and it is nearly always that—of a disgruntled neighbor who thought she'd square off with her for something.

"At any rate, the Immigration officers picked her up. Yes, she was born on the other side...she didn't have any papers to show her entry. Sure, she came over the border illegally, and so forth. So, off she goes to Ellis Island to be deported while three small children sit waiting for her. Her husband at the time was in the hospital with a broken back. It was a pretty serious case, it struck me, and so it did the social worker who ran across the case at Ellis Island and telephoned me about it.

"I sent for Mr. Husband, and I said, 'Mr. Husband, this is terrible. Just look at this case! Now, these are the facts, so I am told. What can we do about it?' He said, 'Well, she is clearly deportable. That's all within the law.' 'Yes, I am sure it is within the law. It sounds just like the way the law reads to me. I am sure it is within the law, but what can we do?' 'Well,' said the old bureaucrat, 'I will see what I can do. I will try.'

"So, he went off, and he was gone about two hours. Meanwhile, I telephoned to the social worker at Ellis Island to comfort the woman, to tell her that she wouldn't be deported tonight, that she would have twenty-four hours' respite.

When Mr. Husband returned with the case, she said, he informed her he had not done anything and that, in fact, it might be better to do nothing.

"My jaw fell," Perkins recalled. "He said, 'You see, you get into so many controversies with the officials all the way down the line when you start to take action. But we can just remand her back to the station in the town where she lives—where she was picked up—for further questioning. Then she won't be on Ellis Island. She will be home where she belongs and where she lives. Then after that, we can take our time.'"

Perkins said she praised him for his ingenious solution.

"'Well,' he said, pulling his chin, 'you know I have been in public life a long time, and I have learned that Man must so administer the laws of men that the laws of God will have a chance to operate, too.'

"I have always thought," Perkins continued, "that from such a simple bureaucratic man—from Vermont, by the way, so perhaps he had some of that old spark of independence left in his nature—that that really was the attitude that ought to be expressed, if not by Mr. Husband and his likes, [then] by the church, so that those who walk down here and take an oath of office, and then go and sit in a petty administrative, quasi-judicial procedure will know that they are dealing with Man, yes, under the laws of the State of New York, but under the laws of God, and that the laws of God must take precedence" adding "that what serves the moral welfare and the moral improvement of these people of society must be observed, and that it is quite as important as the strict letter of some lawyer's interpretation of what some part of the law means."

Pleading for the Moral Law

Assuring her audience that she was not urging that bureaucrats take the law into their own hands, she said, "I am pleading only for a knowledge of the moral law, and a knowledge of the law of God by those who administer the laws of men, and an enthusiasm for the carrying out of those laws and of that attitude."

When asked after the intermission for clarification about what she meant by instruction in Christian principles, she said she was thinking specifically about the individual's relationship to the "order of society," such as government and economic life. She said the doctors of the church from Thomas Aquinas and before had stressed that politics and economics are functions of humankind and that Christians must make sure that the situation does not become one in which humankind is seen as a function of politics or economics.

Commenting on what forms such instruction should take, she said she would not want to see the clergy "feeling for one moment that they must instruct their people in how they should act in a political matter, that is, what political action they should take...or what economic action they should take..." But she said they can "lay down some of these simple principles about what, for instance, the early doctors of the church called a just price. What is a fair relationship between an owner and those who rent his property from him? What control has a man got? I think that St. Thomas Aquinas wrote it out very clearly—that Man's right to own property, to acquire it, and to dispose of it, or to give it away, was absolutely unchallenged but that when it came to the use of his property...it had social implications. And he had a social obligation, that is, an obligation to the rest of his fellowmen to use that property in a way which served the ends of Man, which are a supernatural end; that served the ends of the community for their welfare, for the healthiness of their lives, for the building up of public morals, and for the final movement of Man toward God."

Acknowledging that the clergy do instruct the faithful, she said the long sermon's "passing out of fashion" had handicapped the clergy in their ability to make "available to their people enough of the basic doctrine which relates to [the] laity's obligation to conduct the bank and the store and the manufactory and the bakery and the house and the street cleaning department in a Christian way. I think that it has been lost.

"I ran across the other day a book, a very crude book offered by and sponsored by somebody who teaches in the School of Social Work of Boston College, which is a Jesuit institution in Boston. I think it is called 'Morals (and something) for Public Officers.' But anyhow, it begins and states what is the proper moral attitude and position for a mayor of a city or a town, for an alderman, for a member of a legislature or a senator, for the head of an operating department, for a policeman, and a fireman, for an officer of the court. Well, you'd be surprised. It was very good reading when I got into it. It was pure Thomistic philosophy except that it was put in extremely simple terms.

"A policeman, according to this, should not and must not, as a matter of Christian morals, use force in arresting or apprehending a criminal. No matter how bad the criminal may be, he must not use force beyond that which is barely necessary to apprehend him and take him into custody. Nor must a policeman—and this is very interesting in the light of what we often condone today—misrepresent himself, or an officer of the law in plain clothes. He must not misrepresent himself. He must not be permitted to join an organization—undercover men, we call them—make people believe he is acting in good faith, and then find out those things which he uses to betray them, even, says this pamphlet, if they are evil and wicked men. Nor must an officer of the court obtain testimony from a witness by bribery, corruption, promise of favors, or anything of that sort. Very strong in the City of New York!

"I'm not sponsoring this, and I haven't had a chance to consult any of our clergy about it, but I was fascinated to think that anybody had attempted to write down some simple rules. When I get back to Washington, I am going to read what a public officer ought to do or not do!" she said, invoking laughter among her audience.

After a brief intermission, Perkins joked with her audience about the two written questions she was asked to address.

"Both of them are so hot that I don't know which one to take first. The first one that came to my hand was so difficult that I thought, well, the next one won't be so bad. But the next one is, if anything, a little worse. I will take the first one, which is bad enough."

As the laughter form the audience subsided, she read the question concerning that year's third party Presidential candidate, former Vice President Henry A. Wallace, who had also served in the New Deal first as Secretary of Agriculture and later Secretary of Commerce. Raised as a Republican and a Presbyterian, he had left the church of his youth and explored many different traditions, especially theosophy. He became a Democrat in 1936 and started worshipping at St. James, Capitol

Hill, where Perkins was a fixture throughout the New Deal years. He formally joined the church in 1939.

"We learned in the second lesson 'Blessed are the peacemakers.' Does that have any bearing on Henry Wallace's party of peace?' Another ripple of laughter coursed through the room.

"I think it does, because I think Mr. Wallace, and certainly very large numbers of those who have associated themselves with him at the present time, do believe that they are the only people who are vigorously holding up the standard for peace, a standard to which all good men can repair. So that in their own minds, and their own thinking, the fact that the peacemakers are blessed gives them an understanding of themselves and of their right to make a decision to form a third party— somewhat contrary to the drift of opinion in this room and not so contrary to the drift of opinion in the Middle West, by the way.

" But they feel they have a right to do it and to take what is, after all, a drastic position to separate themselves from the habitual old two parties of this country. And, of course, particularly with Mr. Wallace, he separates himself from a party at whose hands he had had great honors and great political opportunity. I don't know whether you know enough about the way politics is practiced in modern times to know [that] that just isn't done." Her remark again elicited laughter.

"It is very hard to explain," she said, but noted that it led directly into the next thing she had wanted to discuss—the nature of politics and the individual's relationship to it. "And this is it.…politics is a function of Man's nature and activities upon this world, *in* this world. It is necessary for the ordering of the external part of his life."

Politics: A Basic Function of Humankind

"This is the way the doctors of the church have defined it. Politics has charge of the ordering of the external necessities of his life. The original idea is that it keeps order and that it makes a certain adjustment between conflicting interests or people whose interests get in the way of each other," adding that among Christians some such system of political structure is necessary for the development of human life and the maintenance of peace and order. Ultimately, though, "politics comes down to becoming a series of moral choices. This is particularly true in a democracy where the people are sovereign and where the people must say what is to be done about any given set of questions or any given set of proposed activities."

She went on to contrast this concept to life in a monarchy with a benevolent despot who has absolute authority. "He makes all the decisions, and the people acquiesce. If he is properly instructed in the Christian faith, he will not make decisions that are contrary to their moral welfare or to the laws of God. I mean, that was the old theory. But in a democracy, where the people are sovereign, and where the people have not only the right, but the duty, to express themselves with regard to these various proposals for external action in the order of society, the question of what Christians should do becomes very important.

"Now, what I wanted to say was that Christians must regard entrance into politics and political activity as a major, basic Christian duty. And they must enter it as Christians....Even just before an election when it gets hot, they must contribute the Christian attitude. That doesn't necessarily mean a namby-pamby, forgiving attitude toward the man you disagree with, but at least the contribution the Christian makes to a political discussion must be a contribution which points out, in as acceptable terms as possible, what the over-riding laws of God are with regard to this matter.

"Is it a matter of agriculture, for instance, that is being discussed? Then, what are the laws of God with regard to Man's use of the land and the fruits thereof? What's the understanding, and what has been the Christian experience of that? He must bring that to bear upon the political discussion and in his own ability to make up his mind. And in his own ability to make up his mind as to what he should do, he must influence, so far as he can, the party to which he belongs—or the segment or the faction within the party to which he belongs. He must influence, as far as he can, toward a true and right and moral understanding of the political function and of the laws of God as dominating over that political function. And no matter what party he belongs to, that's his obligation.

"Then, of course, he must seek such guidance as he can in his own personal, spiritual life by the utilization of the same spiritual methods which he uses to assist him in the decision of what he should do about any other problem in his life where he has to take an affirmative action, and wants to bring that affirmative action, so near as possible, into harmony with the will of God.

"Now, Christians should do that, and then you look at me and say, 'But do you mean form a Christian party?' And I believe 'no'…that's not only most unwise, but would lead to the very confusions which we strive to avoid. All right, then Christians will pray together. Christians will analyze the political questions before the country in the light of the moral law, and then Christians will do what? They will go and vote in different parties. Is that possible? I think it is. I see no reason why we should not accept that as an appropriate way of exercising the Christian function in politics.

"Each one of us has a different life experience, a different personal experience in the flesh—a somewhat different and more or less developed spiritual experience. Out of his experience in the flesh, he sees certain things. I have seen poverty, and I have seen unrelieved poverty, and I have seen what appeared like hopeless poverty. Therefore, I am bound to be biased in favor of any candidate or any party or any program which will put forth what looks like—what appears to me to be—a practical and sensible program for the relief and prevention and mitigation of that particular kind of poverty."

She suggested that people who had not been exposed to such poverty in the formative period of their lives but who had been exposed to the need to live within their means will see it differently. They might feel that the highest priority would to be to avoid spending more taxpayer monies than the government took in in a given year.

"You can't expect the whole human race to have the same experience at the same time, or any Christians to have it. I think we must come to respect each other's differences of political views, admit their [Christian] basis ...," suggesting that we can "assist each other in the moral and Christian analysis of the political problem even though we don't agree at all with each other on the conclusions. For the failure to analyze the political problem has, I think, led to more bitterness and more partisan dislike than almost any other one thing. "I also think that this attitude on the part of Christians in the way they face their political duties and obligations, either within the party to which they belong or as independent voters, is bound to have a spiritualizing effect on the life and attitude of those who conduct politics on the partisan level…" She said it would also effect the political principles which finally got into circulation and were finally proposed. It would also have the effect of "destroying the cynicism with which so much of our political activity and life is conducted today.

"So, I say that where I analyze the same problem and come out with a view that I have got to support the Democratic Party with regard to this, and my friend, Edward, over here analyzes the problem by the same moral measurements and comes out with the belief that he must support the Republican Party in regard to this, we have both made a contribution, I do believe, to the spiritualizing of the whole political activity of mankind, and to raising the levels upon which the rest of the political people make their judgments and decide their questions, raising those levels into something which can at least be thought of as expressing the relation of man to man, and of man to God."

Turning again to Henry Wallace's third party effort, she said, "…certainly liberty, peace, opportunity, prosperity— everybody is for those, aren't they? I mean, you can't possibly be against those principles. What we really mean is that we don't agree with him in the way in which has chosen to do it, but I do not know. Maybe he may have more influence that way. As for me, I know I will have more influence staying within the party where I already have a position in which I will be consulted on a few things—not many, but a few things that I'm supposed to know about."

This latter comment, no doubt an attempt to be modest, is a major understatement of her influence. She had been the chief social policy advisor to the Democratic Party leader from 1928, when Al Smith was nominated for President, right through the night she was speaking. Smith had appointed her to his cabinet in 1919 and had relied on her as his consultant when he created the state legislature's Factory Investigating Commission in 1911. Arguably, on the night she spoke, she had been the "go to" person on social policy for some thirty-seven years.

"So, I have more influence there, more Christian influence than I would in trying to follow Mr. Wallace. Frankly, I think he has made an error in this reasoning. Perhaps he has included among his premises certain things which are not completely correct, or has omitted from his premises certain aspects of the practice of politics with which he is not familiar, so I couldn't come to the same conclusion that he has. But I think we should respect his attitude and the integrity with which he has proceeded to develop this position. I think…we Christians are bound to come to very different conclusions as to what is the most practical thing we can do, not only in political matters, but in economic matters at the same given time."

On Getting What You Pay For

She interrupted her reading of the second question from the audience to comment. "Has anyone ever suggested to our knowledge," the question began, "that government itself be completely honest, that is Christian—". She challenged the premise, saying, "I wouldn't quite say that they are just the same because I know plenty of God-honest pagans, and the difference between them is that they don't forgive the sinner who is dishonest, and they don't overlook his defects, and they don't expect to give a little more than they get, and that kind of thing."

She then resumed reading the question: "—in the conducting of the government services so that people pay only for what they get and get only what they pay for in their use of the various services operated by the government? This principle seems to be the very basis of all private exchange."

In response, she said, "Well, I hope it is not the basis of all private exchange. I get so much more than I ever pay for, not only out of the government, not only from the government in its general protection of my life and interests, but out of the people I do business with, the people from whom I buy, or who serve me in one way or another. Always, it seems to me, I am getting a little extra, a little more than I bargained for. The 'baker's dozen' was the old name for it. It was a gesture of good will."

She then related a brief anecdote about an experience she had had a few months earlier. "I had to see a man on a bit of business. A couple of rugs had been sent to him by mistake by my tenant, not by me. I had told her to have the rugs cleaned, and if they were worth it, to have them mended and to let me know the price....After a year or so, I got a bill from him for a very large sum of money, and I wrote to know "What was this for?' He said it was for cleaning and mending the rugs. I asked which rugs they were. He told me one of them was a rug for which I had paid on Third Avenue, when it was new, $3.50...It was all worn out when last I had seen it and due to be thrown away.

"At any rate, he said, won't I come to see him? I came to see him. Well, almost as soon as I spoke to him I realized that I was dealing with a man who wanted to do the right thing by me. He had a sense of true justice, of just price, and he strove to find [it]—and, of course, just as soon as he began on that line I strove also to find the just price between us. We had a situation where recognized that the rug never should have been mended and should have been thrown away. I paid half the price for mending it because, after all, some value has been added to it by the mere mending. It can now be used for at least a year.

"So…my life is full of episodes and incidents of people doing for that which they were not requested to do by any contractual obligation, but just out of good will and all that kind of thing. So, I don't know anything about this idea that in private business you only get what you pay for."

She drew laughter from her audience when she said, "My bank, why, the Fifth Avenue bank, worries about me and sends me telegrams if I look as if I were going to overdraw my account. It doesn't do them any good. My little deposit doesn't add to their capital, but they don't want to see me, you know, held up as an example of bankruptcy."

Reverting to a more serious tone, she concluded, "…I can't quite hold that this business of paying for what you get and getting only what you pay for is common in private affairs. And, certainly, I think that whatever people pay for the government services is probably a little less than the services are worth to them. At least, that's been my experience.

"I know there is a school of thought who thinks it is terrible for spinsters and bachelors to have to pay a school tax.…I know that always has arisen in New England protests against having to pay the school tax when you have no children.

"It seems to me that one wishes to live in an orderly society. One wishes to live in an intelligent society. And the price you pay for it is to have some schooling for the younger generation. I should suppose it was extremely simple.

"No, I don't think the government is dishonest. I don't think they charge more for the services than they are worth." She drew laughter again as she concluded her remarks. "Didn't you ever have the experience of the government sending you back 15 cents in stamps that you overpaid? It does happen occasionally."

"Are there any other questions from the floor? Does anybody want to ask me anything about these things I don't know much about? I do want to talk, and I will next week, if all goes well, about Man's—not only his relation to politics, and the relation of religion to politics—but also about Man's function of economic life; his organization of an economy which will support him and those dependent upon him; his organization, operation of an economy which will...produce goods which are needed by the community. Of course, we shall at once get into very difficult modern problems in that field—problems of what is a true economic production. And is there such a thing as its being a sound economy when people produce things that are not needed, that nobody wants, that has [sic] to be forced upon the community by a kind of false and blatant advertising? There are explanations of that which, at least ought to be taken into consideration before an industry is judged as being useless because it does that kind of thing.

"There are all of the problems connected with the understanding of the part that money plays, that just plain money—cash—plays in an economy; and the difference between the money investment in an industry, and the machinery or capital investment in the industry, and the management investment in the industry of brains and knowledge and [expertise], and the labor investment in the industry which consists of the manual dexterity, skill, and labor.

"All those things, of course, go into the intricate and complicated pattern of modern industry," she said but insisted that the same fundamental moral values apply to all the various elements of economic life. She listed them as:

- what constitutes a just price
- what constitutes a fair bargain between employers and their workers
- what constitutes an honorable relationship between the owner and his customers
- what constitutes a fair and true moral relationship between an owner and management of an industry
- what constitutes an honest relationship from whom the owner borrows money or raises capital.

"All these are problems which greatly distress many of our fellow Christians. And as you know, there is a large English school of thought deeply concerned with just these problems. I suppose they might be called the Christendom group, although there are a much larger number of people than those who belong the organized Christendom set. I do think it always pays to read the things that they write. The church newsletter,[27] which comes from London, occasionally has a great deal… about the just price and how price can be restored to terms of justice," she said, noting that there was a special concern in England because the country was in the throes of a great economic upheaval.

The evening ended on a note of humor with her closing remark. "I suppose there are elements in New York City who would like to be able to speak up and say what they think a just price would be with regard to, shall we say, mutton chops or something of that sort," again drawing laughter from her audience.

Above: Outside the Chantry of Grace Church, Broadway, where Perkins married Paul Wilson in 1913. *Below*: The nave of the Church of the Resurrection, E. 74th St., where Perkins was a member from the late 1920s and where her requiem mass was celebrated in 1965.

Chapter Three

On the Vocation of the Laity

The night of February 2, 1948, found much of the northeastern United States blanketed with snow. In the face of life-threatening fuel shortages, the Mayor of New York had assigned observers to fuel trucks to ensure compliance with the city's policy giving priority to domestic uses at the expense of businesses.[28]

In the Long Island community of Port Washington, a dispute over snow removal responsibilities had ended in two tragedies. A woman and three of her children perished in a fire because the firefighters lost critical response time in locating a hydrant under drifts of snow. Within the same 24-hour period, the home of a well-known writer had been leveled in a blaze that was complicated by the same problem.[29]

In this, the second of her St. Bede presentations, Frances Perkins comments on these current events in the context of her belief that the vocation of the laity is to conduct the secular life of the community according to Christian principles.

The mayor, whom Perkins described as "a Christian man," was William O'Dwyer, a Democrat who had failed to win President Roosevelt's endorsement in 1940 when he ran against the Republican and Socialist-endorsed reform mayor, Fiorello LaGuardia. Although O'Dwyer lost that race, he had been successful six years later.

A former district attorney and later a judge, O'Dwyer had built a reputation for compassion in his handling of juvenile offenders, preferring to involve clergy and social workers in problem-solving rather than relying solely on the machinations of the legal system, an approach Perkins could undoubtedly support.[30]

In speaking to her audience, Perkins commends O'Dwyer's decision to support domestic rather than commercial fuel needs as an example of the kinds of moral choices public officials are required to make. She asserts that it is the duty of Christians to make the Christian perspective known.

In this lecture, Perkins distinguishes between the vocation of the laity as it related to the life of the Church—the ecclesiastical/liturgical vocation—and the broader vocation of the Christian in the world. She reiterates her understanding of the Incarnation as the impetus for efforts to build a Christian society, but she develops the concept further by giving examples of what she believes to be a Christian spirit alive in the secular life of society. While she expresses confidence that this spirit is in abundant evidence, she also expresses some frustration that it is not often recognized as such, even by Christians, whom she describes as "shy about claiming too much credit for it."[31]

In a letter to her friend, the Rev. Canon Bernard Iddings Bell, she expressed exasperation about a meeting in which she struggled to get a committee to use the word "God" rather than the vaguer "spiritual values," phrasing apparently preferred by the majority.[32]

Despite her decided preference for Christian terminology, her view is not one of rigid triumphalism, but it will be the final lecture in the series in which she more clearly states her openness to plurality.

Although her resistance to the de-Christianization of American culture may appear dated, her comments on the power of memory, the imaginative function, and the limitations of linear logic seem surprisingly contemporary. They come, however, after more than twelve years of monthly retreats at All Saints Convent in Catonsville, Maryland, and elsewhere, so it is reasonable to suggest that these insights have their source in the sacramental mysticism that informed her spiritual life.

She goes on to detail the thoughts of Canon Bell on the potential of the arts to restore humanity to a knowledge of God. Based on her own interest in art, noted earlier, it seems safe to suggest that Bell speaks for her on this point.

In a draft of a planned review of Bell's book, *A Man Can Live,* Perkins wrote, "Science and reason are accepted and respected, but in art and in religion there lies deliverance. The act of faith lays hold on some meaning which lies beyond science and reason."[33]

As one whose principal achievements were effected through the apparatus of the state, it is not surprising to discover that Perkins holds an affirmative view of the state. She equates Marxism-Leninism with the views of Pelagius, whose views were condemned as heresy in the fifth century because they were thought to deny both original sin and Christian grace. Marx and Lenin both believed the state would eventually wither away as workers gained mastery over their destiny. Humanity, in this view, was ultimately perfectible. Perkins, on the other hand, saw the state as a permanent necessity. In this respect, her views were consistent with Thomas Aquinas, who said the capacity for self-government was a gift from God. Although she does not indicate that she is familiar with it, her affirmative view of the state was also consistent with the sacramental understanding of the state embodied in the Church of England's coronation liturgy, which portrays the monarch as an icon of Christ in his kingly role.[34]

This view is also found in a small pamphlet she used in preparation for the Bede lectures. Entitled *A Christian Realm*, it was published in 1940 by the Church Union in England. The pamphlet asserts that the "state, as the political organization of society, though it is not omnicompetent, has a necessary and divinely sanctioned positive function of its own in human life."[35]

Despite her high view of the state, she does not subscribe to the notion, advanced by some early twentieth century socialists, that all social welfare activity should be initiated by the state. In a speech to the Personnel Research Federation some years earlier, she had commented favorably on the experimentation that was possible only in the private sector.

"Government cannot, I think, ever take the lead in the development of these new experiments," she said. "Government, representing the public in the great mass as it does cannot afford to make the experiments, cannot afford to take the chances and make the discards which are necessary in any laboratory in experimental work. Government will follow behind, but government must furnish a soil favorable to the development of such enterprises."[36]

At a later point in tonight's lecture, she expresses her view that she believes it is possible to be a Christian and be active within a political party that opposes economic planning and government enterprise.

Elsewhere in her presentation, she illustrates her belief that self-awareness is the starting point for Christian vocation. In commenting on groups that come to Washington to testify on public concerns, she expresses a wish that they would spend more time becoming familiar with the realities of their respective local situations. She says it is by working on local concerns that a "true authority" develops. This recommended approach is, of course, the very same approach she used in pursuing her own vocation: starting in the settlement houses, going on to city-wide concerns, then on to state government, and finally the national government.

She would reiterate this theme following her Bede lectures when she spoke at an anniversary dinner of the National Consumers' League the following year. Commenting on the League's work style in the days when she served as staff, she said, "another unique characteristic of the Consumers' League or method, shall we call it, of operation has been its continued insistence that the members of the Consumers' League bear the burden of the work themselves. Now this is really unique in modern social work. I don't know whose idea it was or if it was merely a counsel of great poverty, or that there was no one else to do it. But I suspect it was really a principle that it was understood that the people who made all the fuss about working conditions in the department stores and in the manufacturing establishments would themselves go and find out what those conditions were, would themselves go and beard the owner of the store and factory in his office, would themselves with fear and trembling and shaking hands protest..." She said the "fear and shaking" was because "ladies in those days had not been taught how to make a protest."[37]

The Consumers' League, Perkins notes, was not an organization focused on obtaining better prices or improving product quality. It was instead an attempt by individuals to use their power as consumers to demand fair employment practices and improved working conditions. As staff, Perkins would often outline the remarks, but it was the customer or holder of the charge account who would do the talking.[38]

In tonight's lecture, the linkage between personal spirituality and social responsibility shows up quite clearly in her comments on examination of conscience. She believes the same techniques used for individual self-examination are appropriate to social self-examination, and she recommends that the church stimulate the formation of guilds or sodalities of Christians employed in the same occupation who would collectively examine the moral choices presented in their daily work.[39]

Her suggestion of organized intercessions for the clients or customers of the occupation grouping demonstrates further her ability to move from abstract concepts to practical applications. It was a skill honed over a lifetime of seeking to create the conditions that accord free reign to the will of God.

On the ensuing pages, speaking from her own experiences, Frances Perkins shares her understanding of how individual vocation develops, what fruits it will yield, and what its ultimate destiny must be.

* * *

"Now, we are all familiar—none of us who are churchmen, can fail to be familiar with—the function of the laity in the liturgical life and order of the church. We know that the order of the eucharist is designed for the participation of the people in the offering of the sacrifice, and we say here—we offer ourselves, our souls and bodies to be a holy living sacrifice. This has become a part of our understanding—that no liturgical action is complete without the participation of the laity. This has been one of the great elements of knowledge which our church, I think, has handed on to her children everywhere; that they have no[t] only a function, but that they have a duty to the ecclesiastical life of the church itself.

"But in particular, as we discuss the Christian in the world, and the problems connected with the Christian life in the world as it is today, we must examine in some detail the special vocation of the laity to conduct and carry on the worldly and secular affairs of modern society. For this is a duty which has been particularly laid upon the Christian laity—laid, as a matter of fact, upon" all humankind. Again, using "Man" in the generic sense, Perkins said "we must remind ourselves of what we already know of the doctrine of Man: That God made all men, all mankind—the race of Man—and that to the race of Man is committed the earth and the fruits thereof; and that Man must manage that earth, that land, that production of food, that maintaining of his physical life by the labors which he performs with the land and with the natural resources which God has given him. So that to all mankind there comes a vocation.

"There comes the obligation to conduct the affairs of the world and to maintain in health and decency the people who live in the world. But peculiarly there is what we call, not a function, not an obligation, but a true *vocation* for" the Christian laity "to conduct the affairs of the world—conduct the secular affairs of life—in a Christian way, and according to the laws of God and the Christian principles which we are taught by the church to recognize, to analyze, to imitate, and—with God's help—to apply." She said we must apply them in every function and every activity which naturally fall to the laity.

She said we must not overlook human nature in considering how Christian laypeople should exercise their vocation to the end that "they may come together for the production of greater and more comfortable dwellings and covering and shelter against the storm. In considering these activities we must consider them not as important in themselves, but as important in view of what we know about" human nature.

Alluding to her previous lecture, she said, "We discussed, of course—if I may run over the items—the concept that the Incarnation was the principle, the great and mighty principle upon which we rely for our understanding of Man's function in a Christian society, and of what a Christian society ought to be. We rely on that, and we have had revealed to us through that Incarnation some knowledge of Man as Man and his relation to God…. The opportunity to develop a life fit for the children of God—a world, a society fit for the children of God to live in—comes to us as we meditate on, and come more and more to understand, that great and mighty principle which is presented to us in the Incarnation.

"It becomes in this one world…the realization that in Christ we have the great, the mighty, the overwhelming principle of God and man made one—of God and Man reconciled to each other." Through this realization, she said, we see "Man's possibility to be reconciled to himself, to accept himself, and to go on living with this divine aid which comes to him through the Incarnation.

"It is the reason for Man's effort, it is the cause of Man's effort to build a Christian society. This knowledge of the Incarnation, this fact of the Incarnation, gives to Man the capacity to love his fellow creatures, and to work, to cooperate with God for the establishment of a Christian order of society. A kind of holy society which we conceive to be the will of God who made Man, and taking upon himself our nature, made possible for us to understand what are the almost limitless possibilities for the development of the nature of Man.

"I do want to say one thing at this point, and that is that I believe that many of our handicaps, many of our confusions in going forward with a pattern of a Christian order of society came from what is perhaps a part of the modern world's illness—the constant repetition of 'What's the use? Why should I? How can I, with my extremely limited talents, my limited understanding for any of these great principles, how can I manage to do this? How can I, with my sins, with my obvious faults and effects of nature, how can I possibly make any headway either in the Christian life for myself—and certainly, not in establishing, or helping to establish a Christian order of society for others?'

"I think one of the most common causes for the frustration of which we see all around us at every point is the failure of men and women, when they are still young, to be trained in a technique which makes it possible for them to be reconciled to themselves. No man is ever effective and happy and creative until he has learned to accept himself with the particular nature, the particular characteristics, the particular problems, the particular temptations which he has.

"Some people go through life half ill because they are not beautiful. They go through life uneasy and unwilling to participate because they have a peculiar shyness or modesty. People go through life terrifically unreconciled to themselves because they find it impossible to achieve that which their vanity has said they, as individuals, ought to achieve. For them, if they will but become reconciled to themselves, there lies the greatest opportunity to forget themselves and to live in an activity which is directed to the whole order of society, and to a promotion of those things which assist Man on his way to God.

"We mentioned last week, you remember, some of the great items of social progress which have marked the first half of this century in this particular country and in most of the European societies—great progress in which we call the building of a better social order, a more Christian social order, an order in which there *does* seem to be concern for the health and welfare and the future and the opportunity for all mankind.

An Unrecognized Christian Spirit

"This development has been marked, I think, by a true, if unrecognized Christian spirit. I say 'unrecognized' because, except in the earliest infancy of what we call the organized charitable and social welfare movements, except in those very earliest days, the religious aspect of this function has almost been lost sight of as all men have rushed to support a program of general good-will to their fellows. It has become almost a commonplace of American society today to expect that we shall continue those items which go to build up a Christian order of society, an order in which children are given opportunity to be born in clean and decent circumstances, in which the infant death rate has been reduced by making accessible to all of our community the medical and nursing care, the scientific techniques which serve to keep young children in health.

"We have managed to provide schooling, such as it is, for the great majority, and it is the best we know—it isn't the worst we know—to practically every child born into American life. We have even supplemented in recent years his opportunity for schooling by seeing that he gets a certain amount of decent and proper food. The school lunch was nothing but a Christian recognition of the fact that children, if they are to study and to develop, must get a good square meal once a day. We have gone on through a whole series of tenement house reforms, recognizing that Christian families must have a place to live which is decent and clean and orderly if they are to bring up their children to be members of a Christian order of society. So, we have gone through all the phases to the limitation of the hours of labor that are devised to reduce the fatigue and exhaustion and exploitation which was once current and common. We have practically prohibited child labor in this country.

"We have built up, both by voluntary methods and by legislation," she said, techniques of social insurances which assist people over the worst aspects of life, "to say nothing about our great libraries and our general educational institutions, and our opportunities for the realization of culture, which have been a part, too, of the conscious building of a better social order, a Christian social order. But, for the most part, these items have become so popular in recent years that for some reason or other, Christian people have been shy about claiming too much credit for it, for the results of those activities which have been aimed at the establishment of a Christian order of society.

"For some reason or other, with the coming of this century and its greater sophistication, and the passing out of fashion of the more or less routine, automatic church-going habit, people have become shy about religion, and will say to you over and over again—'Oh, well, I had enough religion when I was a child. My grandmother made us go to church and sit through a long sermon every Sunday. That's all the religion I want.' As that went out of fashion people have been shy about recognizing for the public what the mainsprings of their own moral code might be. Yet back of so many of these expressions of good-will there come, we will say, great endowments that are given as acts of charity, that come out of a complete giving up.

"For instance, the giving up by the Diamond Match Company of its patent on non-phosphorous matches was, I think, one of the greatest examples of Christian good-will and Christian self-sacrifice for the benefit of society that I have ever known."

The event Perkins describes was a significant one in American business and labor history. The use of phosphorous in the manufacture of matches often resulted in a painful disease known as "phossy jaw", which was often fatal. In those instances where it was caught early enough to be treatable, it required removal of portions of the jawbone, resulting in permanent facial disfigurement. Most of the match workers were women.

A "match girls strike" in London in 1888 touched off a campaign to ban the use of white phosphorous in the match industry. By 1901, it had been banned in Great Britain, and by 1906 it was prohibited in international law by the Berne Convention. But white phosphorous remained in use in the United States until 1911, when Diamond Match, which had been licensing its patent for non-phosphorous matches to other manufacturers, voluntarily renounced the patent without compensation. Many of the licensees also renounced their licenses without reimbursement of the fees they had paid to get them, thus paving the way for a federal law to ban the use of phosphorous. *The New York Times* heralded the event with a page one headline, "Match Patent Ended for Humanity's Sake."[40]

Expanding on the significance of the incident, Perkins noted that "even the heirs and assigns of the gentlemen who, then owning and operating the Diamond Match Company, signed away their patents... are shy about saying, 'Yes, father was really a good Christian man. He did it for a Christian reason.' But I happened to be present when it was done, and I know that it was Christian ideals and a Christian sense of right and wrong that made it possible for the Diamond Match Company to say, 'We don't need to make money this way. Let the world have this patent for making non-phosphorous matches, and we will make a living somehow'—a truly Christian attitude toward the social order and... the infinite worth and value of each individual.

"So as one thinks of some of these things one realizes that this Christian spirit has been moving continuously through this century and has established for us in this country and in England, too, and in many parts of Europe, certain patterns of a Christian society which we say are 'economically sound' by which we mean, it doesn't ruin the body politic, it doesn't break the treasury. We still are able to keep on creating new activities which make more goods and new goods and new wealth, and those become a part of our increasing riches."

The Destiny of All People

Perkins then expanded on themes she had developed in the previous presentation—the nature and destiny of the human person: "First, that Man is a creature created in God's image; that as a creature he was made by God as an act of creative love. And this means that God loves him eternally." Because God loves the human race and the individuals in it, she said, the person becomes of "infinite worth and value".

She said, "It has almost become a shibboleth[41] in recent years—and this, I think, really since Hitler taught us to shudder over the violation of these natural rights of Man—it has almost become a shibboleth for people of all religions and no religion to say something about how they believe in the infinite worth and value of every human creature. This is a straight Christian doctrine, and we Christians should be the first to say it, and the first to see that the reason why each man is of infinite worth and value is not that there is anything about him that is lovely or interesting, but that he has value because God loved him, Christ died for him, God made him, God loves him, God endows him, God bestows upon him this value which we recognize and which is a really basic element of any effort which we make to redeem the order of society, or to reform or improve the order of society in which we live."

She then focused on the question of human destiny. "What is the end of Man? What is he about? What is he for?" she asked, then answering with the assertion, "Man is for God. This is the teaching of the church, and all those who have had personal experience, as well as have accepted the divine revelation which came to us from God…know that the destiny of Man and the end of Man is to serve, to love, to know God, and finally, to be joined with him in eternity…," adding that this was the destiny of all humanity, "…not just nice Episcopalians in New York City. It is the destiny of all men and because it is the destiny of all men, each of our own actions, our moral actions, our effective actions in secular life, as well as in the life of the spirit, affect in some way or another the opportunity for all" to move toward their eternal and divine end, "their great destiny", as she put it.

"Then we are taught, too, by the church that Man is endowed with free will, and that in that free will he has the power to choose right and wrong, to know right and wrong; that he gets that out of his nature as a man and that, since he can choose wrong, he sometimes does. This we call sin. He separates himself from God, but he cannot be permanently separated from God if he wishes, if he desires to be united with God; for God loves him when he is degraded and when he is separated from him. Only the deliberate choice to separate oneself from God for eternity can condemn men to a total separation from God.

"So that you and I, recognizing our own sins and our own frequent errors of judgment which separate us from God, must see in every other" person individuals whose destiny is to know and love and serve God, but who may be, in error, in sin, separated from God; but whom we must constantly expect to return, to repent, and to be reunited in that relationship to God...."

She said we also have been taught by the church that sin and redemption are "the principal business of religion" which points out the ways in which we can experience for ourselves "those great and mighty truths" of the redemption of humanity by "the life of our incarnate Lord, his crucifixion, his resurrection, and his application of himself in time and space to those who live now." She added that all sorts of people, even those who have never been taught any religion, apprehend this concept vaguely. "[They] apprehend it and see in each other and in their secular activities even some of this mighty truth.

"I think that the power of the human mind and the qualities of the human mind have been far too long overlooked. We of today tend to think of the human mentality as being—well, you know—the ability to use a system of logic which they used to print in a book. You used to study about the syllogisms and all that sort of thing. This is a great tool, a great and effective technique of analysis of problems; and certainly, no one would wish to be without logic as a tool. But that isn't what men live by. Did you ever know a man or woman to make any serious decisions, such as whom they would marry, by the process of logic? No! They call into play all the other aspects of the mentality for the more serious personal decisions of life, and we have almost forgotten those.

"I think Aristotle calls them the imagetive functions, the imagetive aspects of the mind.[42] These are the image-making powers of the mind. Just imagine that! We live by the images we are able to make within our own mentalities. We guide our lives by them.

"It isn't only the imagination. Memory, itself, is a part of the imagetive aspect of the mentality. What is memory but the making of an image of something not now existing? It doesn't exist today. It's not here and now in this room. But you say to me, 'The house where I was born', or to you, 'The house where you were born'—immediately you have the picture. I mean, it comes to you at once. You could almost go and put your hand on the table, and you know where the dishes are in the cupboard. Your mind is so clear about the things. You say, 'Well, I just remember.' It is an amazing function of the mind—this ability to remember. And what is it? It really is a total recall. It is a recall of truth, for that house *did* exist. That person *did* exist. He is dead now. You recall him. He comes to you in your memory. It is a bringing into this time and this space of events which are true, which have truth, but which are no longer physically present, and physically in relationship to you."

It is by these functions of the mind, she says, that we are "able to apprehend and understand the great mysteries" not only of the Incarnation and Redemption, but "the great mystery of the eucharist whereby there is made manifest to all of us, in a time and space which we are *in*, those mighty truths which are brought from an area where this is no time and space into the time and space which our finite minds are able to *grasp*—not to know *fully*, but to *grasp*."

So, she said, as we think of human destiny and "the moral obligations that rest upon the laity to perform their function for the redemption of the social order. we must, I think, recognize the power of the mind to remember, to make images, to project in an image, to have intuition, which is a kind of flash of knowledge. It isn't related to logic, but is partly memory, partly imagination, partly animal instinct, partly, we will say, spiritual enlightenment.

"The power of the mind to do all those things is what guides us in the project of those elements in a Christian order of society which are possible for us today to understand, to outline, to make into an effective modern program—to implement it, we will say, or to make a project, to make a housing project. How were we able to think about a housing project for some people on Henry Street? Why, it is our imaginations and our memories and our intuitive and instinctive faculties that at once begin to order the rooms and to figure how people will live in this particular kind of building.

"So, it is that any pattern and chart for a Christian order of society calls upon those imagetive faculties of the mind to function. Now, those imagetive faculties of the mind must, of course, be informed by Christian principles. And this is the great duty of the clergy of the church…and of the bishops—to preserve the faith for us, and to teach the faith to us and to our children and our grandchildren, so that we cannot miss it; so that we are not mistaken about what the House of God is, and what God's will for human society is."

She said this understanding was important lest we forget the nature and destiny of the individual and "build a social project that seems to us nice, but which has entirely overlooked the nature of Man and his needs for his life either in the family, or in the society in which he moves; or his life and opportunity to develop as an individual, or his opportunity to develop a religious and spiritual life and function and practice.

Calling on the Highest Function of the Mind

"So, we have to call upon these factors of the mind which are, I really think, not the lowest faculties, but the highest faculties. It has been the fashion in recent years to talk about logic, to think of logic as the highest faculty of Man's mind. I think we need to re-think that. I doubt if it is true. All the creative impulses of Man spring from the imagetive functions and aspects of his mind. Canon [Bernard Iddings] Bell, in this new book of his—which is so interesting, by the way, *A Man Can Live*—goes at great length into that and says that he really seems to believe that out of the group which has seen and experienced life through the arts of writing and poetry, and the graphic arts and of music— that out of that group, if they can but be led to remember what the nature of Man is, they [the arts] can be perhaps the means by which Man, the whole of mankind, or that of mankind which lives in our part of the world, can be brought back to a knowledge of God. He points out how disastrous it is that so many of the modern writers and painters and sculptors have forgotten—if they ever knew—that life is sacred, and that birth and death and marriage—all that goes on in man's life—is sacred." These artists, according to Bell, in forgetting the sacredness of life, "have lost their way in the world; but...they have the type of mind and the type of mentality which can give great gifts to the rest of the more plodding secular leaders who have to carry on the politics and the economics—the work of the world, the day-to-day work with the material things.

"Now, politics, of course, used to be regarded as something that had no part in religion. There used to be a saying, 'Keep politics and religion apart!' You are supposed never to discuss them at the dinner table. I often wonder what they *did* discuss. What is there so interesting as politics and religion—the two most interesting and most compelling, most important subjects, really, with which Man is concerned?" All are concerned with politics, she said. "Aristotle and Aquinas, even William Temple, Archbishop of Canterbury, and Canon [V.A.] Demant—to bring it up to date with recent books—all say the same thing about politics. That it is an essential and permanent function of Man; that Man will always have politics. It is essential to his nature as a man, and for the ordering of his society, of his relationships, each to the other.

"Not all Christians apparently will always believe that. There has been a lot of heresy on the subject, I am told. Pelagius, of course, with his perfectionism, was the great, attractive heretic. Almost everybody in the Anglo-Saxon world really was greatly intrigued by his heresies. There was so much of it that we would love to believe. 'Man is almost perfect and is about to become perfect' is the way it works out. And people would like to believe that.

She said among the more recent examples of heretics who thought the state was not essential and that politics were not a permanent function of human life—that as individuals and society grew better the state would decay and gradually disappear—were Karl Marx and Vladimir Lenin. She characterized them as "very vigorous in their preaching" of the idea.

"There was a very great point made of that—that the state would pass; that it was a temporary arrangement just to get things in order. But it doesn't seem to have passed, does it? And in those countries where they most expect it, where their leaders most expected that every year the state would be less important and politics less of a problem" it seems to become more and more of a "yoke" and more and more a permanent and essential function. She said this growth in importance was all the more reason why it must be blessed.

"It is a permanent function. It can be powerful, and it must, therefore, be a function that is blessed not only by the church, blessed in the eyes of God, devoted and dedicated to God. The dominance of the laws of God over the state and over our economic life and over the whole of society must be asserted over and over and over again."

She reminded them of the long-time public servant who had said, we must so administer the human law in a way that allows the laws of God to operate, too.

"We must keep on saying that to ourselves. We must so administer whatever purely secular function we have to perform in such a way that the laws of God will operate, can operate, are not crowded out and excluded by the artificial restrictions which we apply.

"So it is that within the exercise of the political functions, it is a duty of Christian people to take part in politics. I feel that more sincerely than I can possibly say. The withdrawal of Christian people of high purpose and great nobility of mind and heart—the withdrawal of people like that from political life—has been a terrible loss not only to the world, but particularly to our form and organization of government and society. For a democracy is harder to operate than we'll say, a benevolent monarchy, much harder. It was a hard way of doing things that our ancestors chose when they wrote the Constitution and the Declaration of Independence. The writers and those who drew it up anticipated, certainly, that good Christian men (not women, of course, at that time) would be the first to take their full part in the development of the political activities and in the establishment and maintenance and operation of the state as the political function and exercise of Man in the protection of his order of society.

"The fact that the good Christian people have not done that has left us, I think, in a very peculiar situation. It has left us in a situation where now when a group of partisans and some of their congregation come down to Washington to appear before a committee on some problem, it is usually—I have to say this—international affairs that they choose to come down on. They begin practicing on such small questions as international affairs," she said, drawing laughter from the audience.

"I have always wished and I felt, as I have seen the members of the committee smile, raise their eyebrows as they go out to smoke in the corridors—I have wished that the righteous people would stay home and mind their business."

Perkins said she felt badly about such exasperation because she believed that Christians really *should* do things such as testify before a committee. "I think it is a test of the validity of their faith, and it is a test of their courage that they should do those things even when they don't know much about the subject. But I have often wished that they would begin on some small local project close at home that they could see and upon which they could become informed. It is out of that that authority grows. It is out of knowing what can be done around the block in the adjoining tenement house district, in the enforcement of a decent code of behavior, in the streets in which you live or near where you live—it is that kind of activity in which Christian people and pious people begin to exercise that Christian judgment in the field of politics, out of which they can later develop a true authority if they wish to go to speak to a committee of Congress about some of the greater and more difficult aspects of a problem in international relations.

Taking Politics Seriously

"So that I am always hoping that we shall soon see the time when the Christian people of every community will take their politics seriously, will utilize their knowledge of moral principles and their knowledge of how to analyze a moral problem in applying it to the analysis of the political moral problems which come before the electorate from time to time, and which come before the community in the enforcement or administration of law, and particularly come before us all in proposed legislation. For certainly, if we ought so to administer the laws of Man that the laws of God will have a chance to operate, we should be very careful that the laws that are made by Man are laws which are in the direction of improving and moving Man on towards his great destiny of eternal union with God—to know, to love, and to serve God.

"Every now and then you see an extraordinary item of a Christian order of society, almost unconscious, I am sure. But I couldn't help but think of it as I saw, in the bitter cold yesterday, the policemen riding around on fuel trucks, and saw or heard the wailing and gnashing of teeth that was handed out to us by the movie houses and the theaters and the night clubs and the pin-ball joints. They had no heat. But we realize that the mayor of this city, acting as a Christian man, I am sure, recognized that the maintenance of warmth for families and for sick people was the first and overshadowing duty. Here were the laws of God; here was the will of God having dominance over—yes, he admitted the right of the night club to do business, certainly—that's the way they earn their living. But in an emergency when there wasn't enough heat to go around, the families and the sick must have the heat, and those who made a profit out of keeping the place opened and warm and gay would have to wait.

"I haven't noticed any uprising against that ruling, and yet it was particularly the kind of ruling that is clear and simple to the mind of a Christian man. It seems obvious, but it is not clear to one whose mind is so confused that he believes his duty and his function is to maintain the business of the community, the places of business, and that they come before everything else; that [a] man must make a living first, and the people must wait. The human beings must wait until afterwards. You'd be surprised about the number of people who do get confused about that in politics and in government, as well as in the business life and order of society.

"But I think that we always have to remember what economics and politics are. They were always treated…in the old books as part of moral theology. Economics was defined as that department of moral theology which deals with the way men earn their living; and politics was that department of moral theology which deals with the way men order their society. It is, I think, in the recognition of these two great activities, great functions of Man as part of a moral theology, that we will begin to realize how the law of God can be determined and how it can operate in those fields.

"Now, economics, of course—and we ought to face it—is really nothing much. I mean, there is an awful lot of talk today about the economic law. You'd suppose it was some terrible over-powering thing that had nothing to do with Man, and Man was just a pawn in the field, which, of course, is not true. Very little is known about economics in the first place. It is not a science, certainly. It isn't even a well-constructed, descriptive field of knowledge, because there isn't enough known about it to make it well-constructed. There are whole areas where nobody has written down any figures, and there is no knowledge whatever. All the social sciences, as they call them, are still that way. There is not very much known about it, and we have allowed ourselves to be fooled, I think, by placing so much emphasis upon the great determining factors of economics, and put them down as laws.

"Well, we'll say the law of gravity. It is not even a law like the law of gravity. But I have noticed, haven't you, that for generations, for centuries, Man has been coming to understand the law of gravity, which does seem to be pretty well established as a natural law. He has been understanding it and devising ways by which he can work with the law of gravity and get the law of gravity to work for him, with him, for an end and a purpose. That's what really the development of what we call material civilization has been. It has been Man's understanding of the law of gravity and how to work with it to accomplish human ends.

"So it is, too, with all of this economic information that we know, only half organized. Economics today is merely a description of what men have done in the past with regard to agriculture, agricultural production, with regard to manufacturing and the organizations and distribution of goods, the invention of money as an aid in the distribution of goods. That's all economics is. It is just a description of what men did in the past and what the results have been. Some of them have been very unfortunate. And some of them have been very good; but we can look at it and see that, having been unfortunate, it had better not be repeated.

"You find people today whose concern with economics is to prevent another depression like the depression of [nineteen] twenty-nine and the early thirties. You will find people who are concerned with that aspect of it, are ready to accept almost any nostrum as a human being, unanalyzed, un-thought out, because it is advertised or it is recommended as something that will prevent a depression. You remember that was one of Hitler's great doctrines; that he told us his economic method, whatever it was—fortunately, most of us have forgotten it now—had solved the problem which the Western world was going through, the problem of economic depressions following periods of economic inflation.

The Economy is Made for People, Not People for the Economy

"But if we think of economics as being an instrument, a function of Man, constantly as a part of his moral nature, constantly under the domination of the laws of God, with Man able to choose what he will do and what he had best do for the benefit of the whole of mankind, for the improvement of the life of all mankind, and for the promoting of what we call—for want of a better name—the Kingdom of God on earth.

"Now, I think these aspects of the vocation of the laity, to conduct our politics, to conduct our economic life, are pretty clear. The clergy [are] not going to take that over, nor would they be permitted to. I would like to say this because some of them would make fine political officers, but on the whole I do not believe that the particular talents with which God has endowed our clergy, and the particular training that has been given them, fit them particularly for the performance of the economic and political functions. And that, again, is wished on to us [laity], and we have to do it. We have to take it on.

"Now, can we find out what's right in politics and what's wrong in politics? What's right in economics and what's wrong in our economic activity? Is it at all possible for us to do this? Or have we just got to blunder around and try by experience? Well, I would like to see something tried. I have made little projects at this, myself, from time to time because I have had to make some political decisions. Some of them were extremely hard to make and, you know, the temptation to make the popular decision—the popular decision is very great if you are in political life or in public life. Anyway, that is the great temptation—to do what at the moment is popular, without regard to its realities.

"Well, now, experienced Christians have learned certain things about how to determine right and wrong for themselves. Among other things they have partly learned, not completely, but partly learned the technique of self-analysis—the technique of examining the situation in which they find themselves, and examining their own nature and their own action in the light of some kind of moral code or spiritual rule, which they believe applicable and helpful in helping them to understand the nature of their own actions, the results of their own actions, both spiritually on them, and materially or physically or spiritually upon others.

"Why couldn't we apply some of those principles, some of that method to the analysis of our political and economic problems and decisions? It is not easy, no; but not too hard, either, because we have a certain corps of moral knowledge which we have gained over the ages. The church helps us to gain this kind of spiritual knowledge—the church with her creeds, with her formularies, with the deductive principles which she has taught us to use. To deduce from those creeds and formularies what is an appropriate act or code of behavior in a certain set of circumstances has taught, us I think, a great deal about how to decide what's right and wrong in these fields. People are always asking you, aren't they, and they certainly ask me, 'How do you know right from wrong?' I wish that some learned member of the clergy would write a book on that sometimes; or perhaps it could just be a tract which people would pick up from the porters of churches. But, certainly, people need to be helped to understand on what they base their knowledge of right and wrong.

"Yes, it is a part of Man's nature, and we are taught that Man has some kind of intuitive, instinctive sense of right and wrong, just as he has some kind of intuitive, instinctive feeling about a Divine Being, some external great goodness. This, we are taught and I think our personal experience indicates that it is correct. Our own experience verifies it," she said. We have an instinct for the existence of an outside goodness which we call God, and we also have a kind of inner understanding of right and wrong, she said, insisting that "it is not based wholly upon the animal habits of the community…" There are certain principles we can use in analyzing politics and economics and our own personal behavior, she said. She enumerated resources Christians have for this purpose as follows:

- The holy scriptures, the revelation of the great prophets and teachers
- The pattern and example of the life of our Christ.
- The Ten Commandments
- The direct instructions of Christ to the disciples and apostles to their followers.

"Fortunately, so many of them are recorded and written down where we can read, learn, and understand what they have in mind and what the code of behavior is," she said.

"Then we have the common consent of all the faithful, which has been recorded or established in our creeds and formularies, and the common consent of all those who practiced under these formularies of the church—the thousands, the millions of people who, having practiced under these formularies, say at the end of their life or during their life, or leave it to us as a testament—'Yes, I tried this, and this is the way to know right from wrong' these are the directions that will help you to understand and to comprehend.'

The Examination of Conscience

"And then there is, of course, for the individual, as I believe there must be for the organic society, the direct guidance of God, the direct experience of God achieved through prayer, achieved through meditation, achieved, certainly, by the fellowship of the church, which makes the advice of Christ available to all of us, and particularly the advice and the counsel of the clergy, who are trained and especially set aside to learn and meditate upon these problems of human behavior.

"Are not those same principles of self-examination, the examination by rule of conduct—well, the seven deadly sins is as good as anything. I have often wondered if we started out to examine the moral behavior of our political or economic life by the rule of the seven deadly sins, just as we examine our own consciences, and began with pride as the first of the seven deadly sins, I wonder whether we'd ever get beyond pride in the course of an evening of meditation and examination of our political and economic situation in which we find ourselves.

"Well, of course, I suppose there are some of us who, like myself, say in the examination of one's own conscience, one often doesn't get much beyond pride before night closes in; because it is so much a part of the dominant and underlying mistake and error and confusion of Man. But what happens when you make an examination of the conscience yourself? What have you really done? You have made what the soldier calls 'an estimate of the situation'. You have measured what the field is in which you must operate. You have measured your own capacity. You have measured the mistakes and errors that you have made in relation to the problems that are put before you, and you have, at the end, a good estimate of the situation in your personal battle against evil, and your personal effort to establish for yourself a right and moral and spiritual life.

"Is it not possible to do much the same thing with regard to our society, particularly the political and economic aspects of our society—to make an estimate of the situation by some kind of simple rule of behavior, some kind of simple rule of social order?

"Now, I am hopeful that the next twenty-five to thirty years of this century will show a much greater practice of responsibility on the part of the laity in the discharge of their vocation to order and manage the economic and political and social and educational order and activity of society, for these are the great secular activities which are committed to the hands of the laity. I believe that there is a great opportunity not only for Christian and spiritual growth, but for growth in the field of— what shall we call it—professional morality—in the conscious exercise of Christian judgment in the field in which Christians find themselves called to practice.

"Just think of all the people you know, with the various trades and callings that they follow. They are lawyers and judges. They are doctors and nurses. They are teachers. They are cab drivers. They are railroad men. They are factory laborers. They are farmers. They are cooks. They are all kinds of things. And how many of them in these days are housewives—and a Christian vocation, too, I take it?

"Each of these activities is a Christian vocation to perform in a Christian way. But do we really know—how many lawyers know what is a Christian rule of behavior, a Christian rule to exercise in deciding how to conduct your duties under the law? How many government officials ever think—I think more of them do. You know, it is very curious that a strange sense of responsibility comes over people who are elected to office or appointed to office and take an oath of office while putting their hand on the Bible and swearing, 'So help me God!' A strange sense of responsibility comes over those people who are reminded by that very act—even in the smallest Civil Service positions they take the oath—to whom they owe the first allegiance, and who is the ultimate authority to decide whether they do right or wrong. And who is the ultimate authority in whose name they speak when they perform their functions in conducting the government, even though they conduct it under the strictest laws and rules which our legislature and Civil Service Commission can possibly think?

"But I have long wondered if there would not be a movement among our Christian laity to associate themselves together for the improvement and practice of the Christian life in their particular profession.

"It has been my life experience that men will talk with the highest morality only about the thing they work at, only about their job. About all other things they are superficial, casual, amusing—oh yes!—very quick to pass judgments, very vigorously sometimes, without much knowledge. But they don't talk effectively and responsibly and morally. But you get two steel manufacturers together and ask them questions about the steel industry and what it has done, and what it can do, and how it is financed, and what the labor relations are—what its function in life is—and you will get them talking almost immediately in responsible and moral language. They understand each other. But you ask a shoe manufacturer and a steel operator to talk over questions of even the morals that all employers are supposed to observe, and they can't get beyond first base. They go off in glittering generalities because they didn't know anything about each other's business, and the steel man hesitates to say what it is possible for you to do and what it is right for you to do in the shoe business. He doesn't know. The steel manufacturer doesn't know about putting blotting paper between the two pieces of sole leather and sort of reducing some of the expenses of manufacturers, but not necessarily the price...so he is not in a position to say, 'This is wrong!' But all the shoe manufacturers know that. They know that every one of them is under temptation to do that, and they know it isn't right, and they know why it isn't right. They may not always practice it, but at least they know. They can talk about their moral problem, and they can analyze their moral problem. If you want to get men talking really about the things that are deepest to them, start them off on their jobs. That's another mistaken thing—that you shouldn't talk shop. Shop is the best thing that people do today, and if they work at it and throw their hearts into it, they develop a moral and social response.

Sodalities for Workers and Professional

"I have long thought that if we had—call it a guild, if you want, call it a sodality, call it anything—of physicians, of nurses, of social workers, of lawyers, of judges, of railroad men, of housewives, of anything, coming together, first to try to make a code. 'What's right for us to do? What are our temptations? Let us analyze our special problem!'

"We have different problems from other people in New York, different moral problems, different practical problems. How much must I go in this direction before I can throw my client aside if my client wants me to do the wrong thing? What are the duties of a doctor besides to take care of the immediate needs of the sick? Has he got any other function? Has he got another function to his patients and his clients? Has he got anything to do with their hope of life and their attitude toward the world?

"Well, good moral doctors have. A great doctor, whom I have known for many, many years, when he was a young and struggling man down on the Eastside with an enormous number of terribly poor patients, also had a handful of well-to-do people who had become his patients through one accident or another. Do you know what he used to do? In taking care of the babies in the family, he would say, 'You know, they must have milk and eggs, and so forth'—and the doctor's hand would go into his pocket. 'Go out and buy a dozen eggs! Send the bill for the milk to me, but take two quarts of milk a day.' Then when he was dead broke, when he didn't have any more money left, he would telephone to one or the other of his patients who were a little better off and say, 'You know, Margaret, there was such a nice woman today, and she has two children. They are never going to get through if I don't get better food for them. Would you like to have me send Borden's bill to you?' Margaret would like it very much.

"This doctor, whom we all love so dearly, taught us more about Christian charity functioning through an economic function which he had to perform, and our opportunity to serve through him the great ends of society than almost anything else [he] has ever done. A great Christian attitude, and that doctor was a Jew, a good orthodox Jew who still practices in New York, thank God, and still does much the same thing. In one pocket he puts the money and then takes it out of the other pocket.

"He once gave me a young woman who had had a terrible illness and no place to go to recuperate. She visited me for two months at Harry's suggestion that she needed the country for a while. Why not? Is that not a function of a doctor? Is not the healing of the sick and the healing of the spirit and the relating of the individual to the social life of the community also a part of his function?

Talk about the social worker! I know all about them. Many, many of the modern sins are at high peak in the life of the social workers, whom we have so often been taught to regard, you know, as the modern saints. Not at all! The sin of pride and arrogance and all that sort of thing are just dominant in the life of the social worker who has to know best. You know, she is the one who says she knows what is best for you. 'You put your children in that school, and you send your husband up the river, and maybe I will get a job for you then.' All of the very things that they have to do for the benefit of society breed in them a wrong attitude. And so it is, I think, through all of the activities that we follow.

"You know other professions better than I do, and you will see at once what each profession needs. Why not an order, a society, a club, a group who will meet together, first to explore the problems, to make an estimate of the situation, and to develop the beginnings, the rudimentary moral and ethical code for the Christian practice of that profession or that teaching or that vocation. And then, of course, a great increase in the sacramental life of the group as a method of helping each other and a method of presenting their talents, their skill, to Almighty God…and then, of course, an understanding of the proper relation to the customer, to the patient, to the client, to whomever it is in society. Why not an organized intercession for the clients, for the patients, for the customers, for those who live always under the shadow of this economic activity that may overcome them at any time?

"So…as the laity go on in their effort to carry their responsibilities, there will, of course, come inevitably not only a better understanding of the true vocation of the Christian layman to conduct the affairs of the world under the domination of the laws of God and in a Christian manner, always testing each decision by that, but an understanding gradually of his necessity for a more developed spiritual life…a greater insight into his own nature, and a greater progress toward his divine end, which is his knowledge and love and serving of God, and his progress toward his final end of being joined with him in eternity."

"So, I believe there is a dual action and a dual nature there, which I hope to discuss a little bit next week under the title of the 'The Revival of a Community.' Thank you so much, and if you want to ask me any questions, do; but I have talked far too long," she said to a round of applause.

After a round of applause, she asked, "Does anyone want to heckle me? I use it in the political sense, which merely means, ask a polite question." A member of the audience then commented, "I am afraid that these professional guilds that you are speaking of would tend to be narrow. I am working in a public library, and I'd hate to have an associate of librarians who were just Episcopalians, and just thought about professionals ethics from the Episcopalian point of view, especially when so many people who are not Christians at all have so much higher ethical standards than we do often. Then there is the temptation, especially in library work, to push the Episcopalian [sic] Church to the disadvantage of others. I am afraid that would be augmented by such a set up."

Perkins responded that it was not an act of Christian charity to promote anything to which one adheres to the disadvantage of other people.

"I mean, the first expression of one's love for others is to treat their views and opinions with respect even if one does not share them or thinks that they can be improved. It might be a great exercise for those librarians who are Episcopalian."

Another participant asked, "Isn't it true that the reason that politics and religion are shunned in discussion is because one is not sure what one believes?"

Expressing agreement with the premise, Perkins said, "I think that is a very penetrating statement and very true. It is true that we don't know what we believe about many, many political issues. It is not because we couldn't find out, but it is because we have never thought really, I believe, of the basic Christian principles as they apply to a particular political issue which is up at the moment. Now, we can think of certain things at the time of an election which we would all agree with, things that ought to be canvassed. 'Is the candidate honest?' Well, they always are all honest, you know—at least, so the publicity runs. 'Is he competent? Has he got the training and experience and education to enable him to perform this job?' Yes, that's usually unsurpassable. It is as good as other men's. We don't expect supermen to run for anything. The work of the world and the governing of the world is going to be done by just ordinary men, the way God made them. It is what we have got to contribute as a sense of their obligation and not only to society, but to God, for what they do in office. I think that the issues that are up in each election are perhaps as good a training school, as good an experience in the analysis of moral problems in politics, as anything else would be.

"I think it would be fun for a study group in some parish, or some one of these guilds that I am talking about—I don't expect to see many of them very large ones, but I would like to know there was a center somewhere of lawyers who were practicing to form a moral code, not an ethical code alone, but a moral code which indicated how the laws of God could be followed and applied in this problem. I would like to see a study group of that sort—without the leadership of the clergy, certainly without the dictatorship of the clergy because that is inappropriate—study the moral aspects of the political problems that are up in the next election, we'll say.

"Now, I just don't know what they are going to be. You can't tell what will emerge as an issue between now and next November. But something—they might even do it at St. Bede's! It is a part certainly of the education of the vocation of the community to learn how to think of those problems in such terms. But I do think it is right. We don't talk about it because we don't know, and we evade so many responsibilities under the name of 'ignorance.'"

Another questioner asked, "Are there not some kinds of work today that cannot be done 'to the glory of God'?" Perkins said, "Yes, I think that's absolutely true. That is one of the things that I think the moral analysis of our economic problems ought to bring to us. Many women ought not to be asked to do the kind of work, and to earn a living in the kind of work which is definitely against the moral law, definitely against the laws of God. We all have been through the period when we accepted the dictum, which was very strange when we first heard about it in *Widower's Houses* and *Mrs. Warren's Profession*[43]—that people ought not to profit, you know, from their invested capital in buildings and investments where the land and the improvements on the land were used for obviously illegal and immoral purposes. Or in *Widower's Houses*, where the houses were rotten and decaying and so ancient that they had, in rents, long since paid over twenty times what their original value was in the form of profits," she said.

Building on this concept, she reminded them of a decision of a well-known social activist who had divested of her inheritance for moral reasons. Mary Sanford of Troy, New York, was a Congregationalist who saw socialism as a realization of Christian ethics. She was a member of the League for Industrial Democracy, and her partner, Helen Phelps Stokes, was a co-founder of the American Civil Liberties Union. Sanford had died at the age of eighty-eight less than two months earlier.

She said, "many of us remember seeing Mary Sanford throw back her shares in the great collar and laundry companies of Troy because she had a Christian conviction that she could not take money and profits that were derived from a method of work which she believed was ruining the health of women who worked in those collar factories and laundries. That looked to many people like a ridiculous act, you know, and they always criticized her for it; but it was a true Christian conviction. It made a great impression in New York and made a great impression in Troy. Today you could take the visitor from anywhere, even from Russia, into Troy and show them the collar factories and the great centralized laundry there; and they are a model of all that should be in that kind of industry.

"This all happened in my memory; Mary Sanford did that when I was a young woman." Sanford lived in Greenwich Village during the same period as Perkins and was a part of the activist circles in which Perkins traveled. "I was among those who were terribly startled at so much social conception and so much religious courage," she said.

"Yes, I think there are kinds of labors for which one gets wages, which cannot be done 'to the glory of God.' I think one has to be extraordinarily careful. At this point, the counsel of the clergy, and the advice and consultation of the fellowship of the Christian church, that is, of other people in the church of greater experience, is of essential importance to the individual who often overlooks exactly what line of activity he could take and how he could overcome that evil in which he finds himself sometimes bogged down. But we must be extremely careful, and we must recognize that there are forms of work that cannot be done 'to the glory of God.'

"This, by the way, is a problem that will come up very strongly if ever we launch in this country what we have already taken some steps towards—a permanent program of the prevention of unemployment. Now, the prevention of unemployment is important, and I think we have to do it. I think we have to take it as a moral objective of our economic life, and it will undoubtedly be reinforced by our political life. Already there is a law which gives [a] specially appointed economic council the right to make public reports four times a year, looking towards analyzing the causes and the immediate factors in the economy which might lead to a depression and unemployment, and eventually to recommend action against that.

"When we begin to talk about full employment, about the necessity of having everybody prevent unemployment at all costs, you are going to find people who say, 'Well, you must take this job that is offered'—which, of course, is true, provided that the job is not a job that we would all agree was not only not 'to the glory of God', but against the laws of God, although perhaps not against the laws of the land. And this is a point that is going to be sensitive at some time or other, and Christian people will have to be making up their minds as to what side to support. Must a man go to work in the job to which he is referred if it is a job which degrades young people, we will say? If he gets a chance in a publishing house where they are publishing obscene literature, which is distributed surreptitiously, should we make him take that job? What should we do? This is a moral question in which all of us will be involved."

Another participant asked, "Why do we so often find such reactionary economic ideas among the people who are the most faithful church goers?"

Perkins readily responded, "You find them among people who aren't faithful church goers, too. I think reactionary economic ideas are just the result of, first, true ignorance of the economic world in which they operate. Secondly, church goers are quite capable of sins of greed and covetousness, and so forth; and a good many of us are able to blind ourselves for a long, long time to those aspects of our own personal greed that would be inconvenient if we ruled them out. Of course, I think it is wonderful that they go to church because some day, somewhere, they are either going to hear a person innocently drop a word from the pulpit that stirs them all up, or they are going, on some great, glorious Easter morning, to appreciate suddenly what the redemption of Man means, and how horrifying their own sin of greed is.

"They are going to look deeply into the human heart. It can't be helped. If you go to church enough, you finally get something rubbed off. I have a relative who is always hot and bothered about the hypocrites who go to church. 'They don't lead Christian lives." I always say to him, 'So what! You show me a Christian life tomorrow, and then we will talk about the others.' So many of us want other people to live a Christian life, by which we mean a life that does not give us inconvenience, but may not be spiritual at all."

Another questioner asked, "Could you tell us the views of Pelagius?"

Perkins then responded, "I don't think it would be good for me to give a full exposition of his views. One of his principles, at least as I understand it—and this is very attractive—is that if people did good things, you know, the good pagan; if they did what was kind and good, if they gave to charity and they took care of the sick and the poor, that nothing else was necessary for their salvation. At least, that was the perfecting element in their natures, and so forth, and so on. But you can find out about him in the *Encyclopedia Britannica* at great length. But it was along that same line of what so many secular people call a Christian life.

"Now, how often when somebody dies and they put in the paper how much money he gave to this and that and the other charity, and what good works he did, and how many hospitals he was chairman of the board for, and all that—the cab driver and half the other people you meet will say, 'I guess he was a good Christian man.' But frequently, he didn't know what the Christian principles meant from the point of view of a truly spiritual life, and he died ignorant of the nature of God and of his relationship to him. And the goodness and kindness which he displayed may have been just a particularly amiable disposition or good digestion.

"But, at any rate, we do know enough to know that that is not the answer, and that humanitarianism is never enough. Not only is it not enough for the developing of the man's own soul, but it is not enough to establish this divine end to which he struggles because he does not know and love God, even though he may do those things, in the service of God's children, which are of infinite use to them. But he has been blinded and he has been deprived of that which he, as a man, is entitled to have if he does not know and love God and enjoy the love of God, which is meant for Man's salvation and strengthening."

Can Christians Support Free Enterprise?

The next questioner asked, "Would you say that a Christian could possibly act as such in a society or political party which was based on the principle that 'free enterprise' is part of God's plan, and that planned economy is communistic'?"

Perkins said, "Oh, yes, I think a Christian could exist in that political party, because these are just notions which at one time or another have a kind of intellectual fashion. Many people, of course, are a little bit short-sighted. D.G. Peck, who has written an extraordinarily good book called, *A Catholic Order of Society*—it is good because it is neatly digested, and you can read it quickly, and it is thin, and it is all there—says that we must remember always that there is nothing of particular virtue either about a collective system of operating our economy, or a cooperative system of operating our economy, or a capitalistic system of operating our economy. The test of the virtue, the test of what ought to be done about it, is whether or not it serves the people who depend upon it for the goods which they need, and for the distribution of goods which they need and whether it contributes to the moral spiritual development of men to know, love, and serve God.

"I think we have got to recognize something there is so much talk about. Nobody knows what 'free enterprise' is, and you couldn't get anybody in this audience to go out and start a 'free enterprise' tomorrow; yet we talk a great deal about it. We like it. It suits our way of doing things, and it has worked out very well. But, for instance, if you lived on an island that had an extraordinarily limited soil, we will say, and therefore a very, very limited opportunity of having a decent food supply, such as some of the rice economy islands of this world are, you know, there doesn't seem to be anything remarkable about 'free enterprise' there. The common holding of the rice property, the land that raises the rice, is the most natural thing in the world. There is so little of it; there is so little food that can be produced anyhow. There are so many people. Here again, in a community like that, they work from sun to sun. Child labor laws of the U.S.A. and the hours of labor and the minimum wage just can't be thought of as applying to a community in which the ability to live at all, to eat at all, is based upon everybody's working all of the time. The preciousness of this land that raises their food is so great that to allow it to be exploited under 'free enterprise' is unthinkable.

"As a matter of fact, savage people never do that kind of thing. There are areas of our economy where the common ownership by society rather than by an individual seems to be indicated. Nobody has a word to say about the desirability of the whole atomic energy program, both of research, manufacture, and exploration, being in public rather than in private hands.

"We hardly trust our government with it, but we think there is a chance of a public body utilizing this for the welfare, and not against the welfare of society. So, there are other areas where the cooperative method of doing things is just natural.

"I happen to belong to a town [Newcastle, Maine] which has had a communist economy in one respect ever since the town was founded, I guess, which was about 1700. This is a communist economy in ownership of fish, of all things. The fish that come up the river to spawn in the fresh water, and leave the falls at the head of the tide into the fresh water pond where they spawn are known as alewives. If caught at the proper season, and properly smoked and salted, they become almost as good as the kippered herring. They are in the nature of a kippered herring.

"Well, at any rate, since the earliest times the people of this community have recognized the fish as being basic apparently to their whole economy. While they were farmers and ship builders and seafaring men and fishermen, to get control of the fish stream by one man would have been unthinkable. So as soon as they learned about the habits of the fish, and that you could smoke them and preserve them and sell them overseas even, sell them in lots of places, right away it seemed to be that this would be cheating the whole community out of their fish. They passed resolutions in the town meeting, therefore, which made this common property.

"You can see the degree to which it is communistic. Since the beginning of time every widow in the community, whether she is old or young, rich or poor, gets one hundred fish free, all smoked. The town smokes them and gives them to her. But that is because she is a widow and can't come out with her pitchfork and push the fish, as they come out over the falls, into barrels.

"Of course, the day of not paying people to do it is over. They used to do it themselves. Now they pay people to smoke them in the little smoke houses. But the town owns the fish, and the town sells the fish. And that is why we don't pay as much taxes down there, and I am able to hold on to my own property without being taxed out of creation.

"But it shows that there is absolutely no conflict between a proper and quite capitalistic attitude toward ordinary economy and 'free enterprise', and a communist economy—about one or two things that just seem appropriate for that way of doing it.

"Yes, I think that we are going to hear a lot of talk about planned economy and 'free enterprise', and I don't think that there is anything antagonistic in them, myself. I think that we'll have a great deal of planning under a 'free enterprise' system, and already you know it is the men who have been the most successful in 'free enterprise', reformed capitalism. It has been reformed partly by law and partly by custom and partly by voluntary action. It is very interesting, but many of the people who have been most successful are most interested. For instance, this Economic Council, which is really making an economic plan for the country—it is a project in seeing whether or not a public research body can make, can discover and lay out, certain facts and certain principles of economic activity, and point out ways of developing new projects and new enterprises, and of cutting out certain others that are declining—and recommending (not force), but *recommending*. Whether or not there is enough good sense and moral courage on the part of the community to take that recommendation, I am discouraged somewhat by what I read in the Kiplinger Letter this week. These recent recommendations, which have been made by the Economic Council, are certainly not very drastic."

She said they were "just first steps" which recommended that Congress do certain things, that manufacturers do certain other things, and that merchants reduce their prices.

"Of course, that would not be popular, but they recommend that. Kiplinger repeats their recommendations and says, 'Here is what people might do. All of these classes, if they were well advised as to their real interests, would do just these things.' But he adds cynically, 'There is very little chance they will.'

"Well, I think it is the beginning, and I think you may get a combination there that will be good in the long run."

Occupational Representation in Government

Perkins was also asked if she thought "representation in government on the basis of occupation would provide a better structure for effective Christian citizenship?'

She expanded on the question: "Do I think that to provide in the legislatures of the states and of the federal government a representation not by geographical location and on the basis of numerical representation, but provide a representative from, we will say, each of the major occupations and professions—a manufacturer, I suppose, elected by a manufacturers' association, a farmer elected by some agricultural society, a lawyer recommended by or elected by the Bar Association, and so forth and so on.

"No, I regard that form with horror—not because the Soviets have it either—because when I first read about it as the principle of Soviet representation, I thought it was very good. It was a very good many years ago, and I hadn't seen as much of life then. But it sounded like something very practical because I had seen people in the legislature who, I thought, didn't really know what they were talking about. And I thought, 'Well, in this case they will know what they are talking about.'

"But I think that we do not realize that the questions that come before legislatures are questions which really demand a moral representation of whole cross-sections of society...."

She said in a controlled system, such as the (now former) Soviet Union, would lead to "a terrific number of conflicts and quarrels and double dealing, and groups making common cause—the lawyers and the farmers ganging up on the manufacturers or the merchants, and all that sort of thing. The self-interest involved is so great that I don't think you would ever get that true cultural representation of [a] cross-section of the country, which is what you need. And you need it also for the education of the politician and the representative so that he may know the people and be, therefore, more truly representative. I think it would be very narrowing and, on the whole, very damaging to our free and increasingly responsible society."

She then read a question handed to her on a notecard. "Well, here is a question, and I have got another one much like it in my own mind. 'How might a Christian member of a community act to forestall such a tragedy as the burning of four small children because the town fathers could not agree as to whose responsibility it was to unfreeze the fire hydrants?'

"Here, of course, is a perfect frustration. The deed is done. It is over. The disagreement between the members of the town council should never have taken place, and the man who was willing to unfreeze the hydrants, whether it was his duty to or not, is the one who should have unfrozen them because of the emergency. But he didn't know that apparently. Or, you know, jurisdictional disputes are very serious with people who think it is my job to do that, and are sometimes quite unwilling that other people should do that particular thing. But here you have got something which, having happened, you can't forestall; but what you can forestall is another occurrence of the same sort due to divided responsibility and lack of authority.

"If this is truly a town and not a great municipal community, there is always the board of select men or the town council or town meeting; and certainly, the Christians of that community should see to it—and they can—that a town meeting is called, or that the town council meets…and that not only a resolution, but an actual chart of division of responsibility is set up. Moreover, if it was the duty of one of these men and he did not do it, I think that it is a part of Christian responsibility to find some way of making that clear to him—that he is the one whom the community blames.

"Now, whether there is a criminality attached to it or not is another matter. But there is a moral obligation and a moral responsibility which he hasn't fulfilled, and which I think should be made clear to him. But I think that the most you can do in a case like that is, in memory of the four children and while feeling is hot about it, to see to it that delegation of authority is established in such a way that it can't happen again.

"One of the greatest community projects that this town ever saw was after the great Triangle fire when one hundred forty-seven people were burned. When they met the next day (I think it was on a Saturday they were burned) on Sunday afternoon there was a meeting that filled Carnegie Hall, which was then the largest place available. It was an outpouring of real sympathy and real distress, real sadness, real self-accusation that we have done these things to these young people. There was really a great revival of a sense that this could not happen again, must never happen again; and sort of in a memorial to those who died there was a movement started, which resulted in tremendous improvement in the fire prevention techniques of this town and for the whole state, for fire prevention in the factories. That, I always have thought, was a direct response and a right response to a tragedy which, once it was over, couldn't be prevented.

"Now, I want to ask you another question, because this story was told me today, and it is not unlike another one I know. A school in a very excellent community in New Jersey, one of the most intellectual and cultivated communities in New Jersey, Junior High, I believe, had a theft the other day. It was a very, very stormy day, one of those very cold and stormy days. The doors were locked from the outside. Nobody could enter the school. When the little boy in questions was given permission to go home early for some reason or other, and he went down to his locker to get his things—his rubbers, his boots, his long pants, his warm coat, his cap, his scarf—they were gone. They weren't there. He rushed to tell his teacher. His teacher went down and looked the place over; looked in all the other lockers and couldn't find anything. They reported it to the principal. It was pretty distressing, but what do you think the principal decided? the principal said, 'Well, I can't help it. Get along home!' So he dismissed the school and sent the boy home.

"What do you think he should have done? Is that a right way to go ahead in a Christian community, in a public school? I was horrified by this story. It just seemed to me that it couldn't be. Somebody in that school had stolen the little boy's coat and cap and everything else. And not only was it a dreadful thing for him to steal, but it was a cruel thing to take a child's warm clothing in the midst of a storm. Everybody in the school, of course, was offended, was hurt, was damaged in his own personality, and should have been made to feel so. But this, of course, is what secular education has come to.

"You remember the story of the little 13-year-old girl who, in a school where they had a rule against wearing slacks to school, wore slacks to school. It was in all the papers for three or four days. It was like a flag pole sitting. Everybody was so interested to see who would win. But this little girl wore slacks to school against the rule, and she was sent home. She wore them again, and she was sent home. Her father protested, and then her father aroused the neighbors, and the neighbors' children and all the other girls in the school stayed home from school and walked up and down in front of the school with slacks on as a protest. The principal, when last I read the paper, was still holding out;

and he wasn't going to permit her to come to school unless she obeyed the rules.

"But this, of course, is a part of the—shall I say 'incompetence', the misunderstanding of the function of education; and of the relationships of the children to the whole community and their school; and certainly, some advantages must be taken of that.

"I propose to discuss education a little bit next week as part of the community project. Thank you so much for your patience," she said to a final round of applause.

Above: St. James, Capitol Hill (now St. Monica & St. James), the Washington parish of Frances Perkins. *Below*: The Maryland convent where she spent one day per month in silent retreat throughout her twelve years in the New Deal.

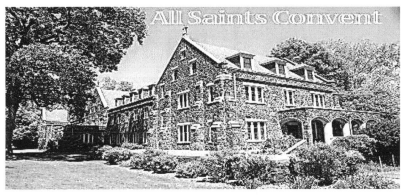

Chapter Four

The Good Life, Community and Individual

Despite the Pope's call for a ban on the atom bomb on February 9, 1948, this event escapes specific commentary in the third and final lecture Frances Perkins delivered as part of the St. Bede series.[44]

The general thrust of this presentation is to establish the concept that the end purpose of humankind is union with God. All human activity must ultimately move humanity toward that end, in Perkins' view.

In developing this concept, she lays particular emphasis on the need for individual reconciliation as a prerequisite for any concept of social reconciliation. She identifies an honest, humble self-acceptance as the first step in creating a social order than can be described as a "Christian" society, one in which Christian principles are realized and Christian ideals can flourish.

She also states clearly her belief that sin is nothing more than separation from God, and that any behavior or situation can be judged by that criterion alone.

She then goes on to suggest that this self-examination can also be done on a social scale by asking the question: "What has a community done to cause separation from God?"

In commenting on the specifics of the latter, she again reveals a sacramental or materialist understanding of Christian principles. Supporting concepts that move our fellow citizens toward God means assuring the provision of good houses and reasonable wages. But she returns to the concept that individuals must first move themselves toward God in a spiritual sense, stressing her view that humanitarian good works in and of themselves are not sufficient.

Here, in the last of her Bede presentations, Perkins translates the ideal of union with God into the specifics of spiritual discipline, asserting that Christians must daily practice the presence of God. She notes that this discipline is not customarily discussed in the context of social obligation. Nonetheless, it is the context in which she believes all love of humanity begins.

Her view of self-acceptance as a kind of compassionate self-love—one that requires patient nurturance—is developed most fully at this point. She suggests that Christians must first assert that Christ is King and then examine their consciences from that standpoint.

Consistent with her understanding of the need for nurturance, she cites both auricular confession (confession to a priest) and devotional manuals as useful aids in the quest for self-assessment and self-acceptance. Her presentation makes clear that she used both of these approaches in her own spiritual life. Although her language conveys the flavor of obedience to the church, her own history suggests that the decision to move in this direction was her own, one based on an assessment that such spiritual exercises were genuinely useful.

Her support of the concept of a "manual" to aid in examination of conscience further illustrates her belief in the inadequacy of the individual as a moral agent. She notes how easy it is to become overwhelmed by it all and suggests that there are times when we are simply too tired to think clearly and need something other than our own judgment to carry us.

That she genuinely believed in this approach was confirmed by the late Rev. Charles Owen Moore, who was her spiritual director in the last years of her life.

"She led a disciplined spiritual life," he said, which he saw as the foundation that enabled her to have profound influence on American society.[45]

Moore, a graduate of New York's General Theological Seminary, had served as curate at Manhattan's Church of the Resurrection from 1959 to 1962, where Perkins had been a member for more than thirty years.

This apparently sincere appreciation of the church and its discipline as a help to her work for social justice appears to be in marked contrast to another churchwoman committed to social justice, Wellesley professor Vida Scudder. A life-long socialist and Anglo-Catholic, Scudder had played a pivotal role in the creation of the Episcopal Church's national Department of Christian Social Relations in 1919.[46]

In an article clipped form *The Living Church* magazine, which Perkins used as source material for her 1941 speech before the Catholic Committee of the South, Scudder expresses exasperation with the deficient social thinking of most Anglo-Catholics in the United Sates. She garners support for her view by quoting British churchman D.A. Mackinnon, who paraphrased Jesus in a prayer, "Father, if it be possible, let this church pass from me." Scudder voices her agreement by asserting that "the only apologetic which has the least hope of being persuasive is 'one which will admit that the church is a question and a scandal.'"[47]

Scudder's remarks reflected the view of many, including some Roman Catholic scholars, that Anglo-Catholicism was primarily an aesthetic movement concerned with liturgical embellishment and virtually blind to the social implications of the sacraments. No such indictment can be found in any of Perkins' comments on the church. In fact, her primary point of agreement with Scudder is probably found in the portion of the article which she herself underlined in pencil, wherein W.G. Peck is quoted on the need to recover "the mediaeval conviction that 'economic action takes place for the satisfaction of the needs of Man considered as a creature intended for the vision of God.'"[48]

A similar statement appears in the Church Union pamphlet, identified in the previous chapter as source material for her St. Bede presentations.

"There is a catholic tradition in this matter," the pamphlet states, "which must be recovered and re-applied to the circumstances of our age. Its basis is indicated by the saying of St. Antoninus of Florence that production is for Man, not Man for production. Only a social philosophy which directs men and societies once more to their true end in God can restore a social order in which men (not goods) are primary and which can therefore preserve the dignity of each human person."[49]

That Perkins would focus on this concept in her reading of Scudder's article is not surprising, given her very explicit exposition of this view in her first Bede lecture. If she agreed with Scudder or MacKinnon's criticism of the church at all, it does not appear in her recorded public comments. It is quite possible that she did not agree, especially in light of what she told Canon Bell in her letter noted earlier about understanding herself as a "learner" in relation to the church.

Her essentially affirmative view of the church and its discipline may account for some of her previously mentioned discomfort with encroaching secularism and an increasing unwillingness in public life to name Christian principles as such. The tension between her Christian identity and her affirmation of pluralism surfaces again in this lecture when she is asked to comment on the removal of religious education from the public schools.

Perkins views this development as a mistake and states frankly that she disagrees with her Jewish colleagues that religious education in the public schools is divisive. Yet, in response to a subsequent question, she asserts her belief that Christians are obligated to cooperate with all others who wish to bring about a "decent" society.

Noting that the Quakers "have not followed with us all of the conceptions of the purpose and function and divine establishment of the church," she goes on to say that "we can learn so much from people like that, people, although they do not agree with us at every point, nevertheless have, out of their own experience, so much to give that we cannot afford to avoid it."

Her statement welcomes the insights of those who reject the catholic vision she affirms, while revealing her understanding that it is the church which leads. Others may follow along a different path, but they *follow* nonetheless.

This understanding was quite likely influenced or reinforced by the idea of the Episcopal Church as a "leadership culture." This idea was the principal driving force behind the founding of Groton, where FDR was educated, and its brother institutions, Middlesex and St. Paul's schools.

It was also advanced by a key member of the church's Board of Religious Education, one-time senator from Pennsylvania, George Wharton Pepper, who told the General Convention "what we must aim at is not systems but men; not literature but leaders. This church is in a position of peculiar responsibility and advantage in the matter of training the leaders in the educational work of the country. Whatever our defects as a church may be, we have the priceless heritage of an inclusive conception of Christianity."[50] An "inclusive conception", that is to say a "catholic conception", and an English-language liturgy were key elements of the advantage Pepper and many others saw.

But Perkins' own understanding was also influenced by the self-understanding of many within the Church of England during this period. As they saw it, the church was a leader of established culture and a primary agent of visionary and interpretive moral construction. Others might dissent from its teaching or decline to participate in its rites, but they were still a part of the culture and society which it headed.

Clear evidence that this view had some degree of acceptance in the Church of England at this time is again found in the Church Union pamphlet. The church, it asserts, "is bound to point out that the nation [England] is living on the spiritual and moral capital accumulated through centuries of Christian teaching and worship."[51]

This concept is reiterated by W.G. Peck in his book *The Social Implications of the Oxford Movement*. The very universality of the scope of the gospel, he says, "the very humanism implicit in the dogmas of Incarnation and Redemption, must eventually bring the church upon the open stage of the world's affairs. There was a profound validity in the Mediaeval attitude. Sovereignty is in the very soul of the church."[52]

Peck states that in spite of itself, "this world bears some marks which would not be there but for the age-long presence of the church; and not even modern vulgarism and 'mass-mindedness' can wipe out the influence of two thousand years." He goes on to assert that, despite the "widening distance between the vision of the church and the aims of the world", the people of the church must "continue to do business in New York and

London, because the world's life, the actuality of New York and London, is claimed by Christ."[53]

Claiming the world for Christ, whether or not the world acknowledges the claim for what it is, is at the heart of Perkins' idea of the vocation of the laity.

How this claiming of the world translates into specific approaches to public policy is explained in response to a question about unemployment. Perkins advocates a number of approaches which she characterizes as compatible with the Christian conscience. They are noteworthy here primarily because they have now been widely adopted by most modern economies to mitigate the impact of cyclical downturns in employment.

Her comment on Social Security benefits is a good example of how her mind worked. She sees, and encourages others to see, Christian concern for the aged at work in the secular system that has been created. In this statement lies the defense of the claim that her life was dedicated to making works of mercy available.

In response to another question, she provides more information on the Christendom group in England, which she mentioned in passing at the end of her first lecture. The group was a collection of writers closely allied with the Anglo-Catholic Summer School of Christian Sociology described in Chapter One.

The Summer School began in 1925 and continued for several decades. Although it was Anglo-Catholic in both in terms of its leadership and its content, its speakers drew on a wider circle. *Christendom* was a journal edited by the English sociologist, Maurice Reckitt, which reported many of the views of both the Summer School and the "Christendom group". Oxford historian Geoffrey Rowell asserted that the two groups had a significant impact on Anglican social thinking. [54] Vida Scudder said the thinking of the group was similar to the thought of French philosopher and socialist Jacques Maritain.[55]

It is clear from her comments as well as the materials found in her preparatory notes that the Christendom group was a primary source for Perkin's own social thinking. Personalities such as Walter Rauschenbusch and Harry Emerson Fosdick, usually cited as exemplars of the Social Gospel Movement in the United States, do not surface in any of her speeches or preparatory materials. No doubt she would have found them "too Protestant" in character.

Reckitt, the *Christendom* editor, expressed such a sentiment himself in his book *Faith and Society*, which drew heavily on the analysis of church historian W.A. Visser't Hooft. Revealing his own disenchantment with American Protestantism's enthusiasm for Prohibition (something the Episcopal Church did not share), Reckitt said the Social Gospel contained elements of narrowness and self-sufficiency and noted that Rauschenbusch had rejected sacramentalism as a parasitic growth on the body of Christianity.[56] Reckitt suggested the United States needed to "open its mind wide to the treasures of social tradition accumulated by Christianity in the days before America offered its asylum to Puritanism..."[57]

Toward the end of this lecture, Perkins expresses sympathy with T.S. Eliot's contention that creating a Christian order of society does not require a substantial number of Christians. What is needed, in her view, is a corps of individuals who experience a relationship of unity with God.

This concept was to show up again in slightly different form in her Consumer's League anniversary speech in December of 1949.

"You remember what Toynbee said," she reminded league members, "about the capacity of a creative minority 'to turn the tide and to keep a whole race from the path of destruction and set it on the path to glory.' That, I think, is what is a part of the duty of this still small and meager, but strong and effective organization."[58]

The organizational reference was to the Consumer's League, but in the last of her St. Bede presentations, she shows that she clearly understands herself and the church to be a part of that creative minority.

The Good Life

On that cold night in February of 1948, Frances Perkins gave voice to the creative minority of which she was such a vital part. She began her remarks noting that she had been "very much interested and very much intrigued by the opportunity for study and meditation and thinking about the problems that are evoked by the title, 'The Christian in the Word.' So, I want to say to the people who are trustees and managers of St. Bede's Library that I am grateful to them for having asked me to come and to say a few words about my own experience in this field.

"And I am grateful to the group who have come for the last two or three weeks, for their participation, for their questions, and for their concentration in helping me to understand for myself what are some of the problems that surround the Christian in the world in the year 1948. For that has been the overall subject, and that has been the project upon which we have all sort of concentrated our minds.

"We have tried in the last few weeks to outline some of the problems that are common to all people who think about the Christian in the world. We have tried to outline some of the problems that have to do with the Christian order of society. We have tried to outline some of the problems that arise necessarily when one thinks of the vocation or the responsibility of the lay people…who are just common people like you and me; who are

Christians, who are devoted, who derive our...inspiration from the church, and what small vision of God we have had, we have had under the direction of the church.

"As we have tried to conceive of what the vocation of the laity is, I have tried to discuss those problems which related to the particular vocation—the special vocation of the laity. I am going to participate in the liturgical worship in the church...in the sacrificial offering of all of the hearts and minds and talents, our souls [and] bodies—all that we have—to Almighty God in the liturgy. But to concentrate particularly upon those aspects of the offering of the laity which have to do with their special vocation which, I think, is the vocation to conduct the affairs of the world in a Christian spirit and from a Christian point of view.

"For obviously, in these modern times when civilization has become so dispersed and so varied that all people participate and take part in, and share some of the benefits and advantages of civilization, certainly the laity and not the clergy have the responsibility for the conduct of our secular affairs: our affairs of banking and finance, our affairs of state, our affairs of government responsibilities, our responsibilities in the economic world, in the political world, our responsibilities in the social and cultural fields. For it is the laity, and not the clergy, who conduct our musical life, our literary life, who set their seal and put their criteria—their Christian critique—upon the questions of when is the drama, when is the literary product of our community an advantage and an asset to the Christian world.

"So, I have been very much interested in canvassing with you in these last few weeks some of the problems that surround the questions of the significance of the laity in the Christian community. And tonight, by virtue of the fact that I have had to— you know, you have to write out, oh! months in advance, a little outline of what you think you are going to say—by virtue of that, we had a subject set for tonight which was not only under the general classification of the Christian in the world, but which concentrated upon the conception of what is a good life both for the community and for the Christian individual. I suppose that means: How can we organize ourselves? How can we direct ourselves so that both the community— the Christian community and the individuals in it—can for themselves obtain or approach this good life?

"Now, we have tried in these last few weeks—at least, I have tried, and I hope some of you have tried with me—to present the significance in the terms of this world, of the principle, of the great mystery of the Incarnation. I have repeated over and over again, and I fear to the point of boredom, that it is the fact that God became incarnate in a human form and with a human mind and spirit, in human nature—that God became incarnate in human nature—that it is that fact, that great mystery and yet that great fact that makes it possible for us to think in terms of a Christian social order."

She said that nothing else could challenge "our respect, our concern, our obligation to the people who live with us and live around us." God became human. God created us in his own image. God loves us. "God is present eternally and forever, now and in time and space, eternally in his Incarnation in the form of our Lord and Savior Jesus Christ," she said.

"It is because of this terrific mystery—this almost incomprehensible mystery of the Incarnation—that we human beings not only regard our brothers, but regard ourselves, regard our individual selves, as within the pattern and purpose of God's plan for Man on earth. The Incarnation has been extended as we know to all mankind, and we accept that, in every aspect of mankind's life. When I was a child and people said, 'Oh, well, you know the Incarnation means that God has extended himself into all parts of the earth,' I always thought of China and the islands of the sea. As I grew older, I realized that that meant God had extended himself into the sins and difficulties and disorders and chaos of New York City and Boston and the life of the Perkins family and to me. This is what really the Incarnation means—that God has planted himself, has extended himself to be a part of all of the life of mankind, even to the life of people like ourselves—you and me," she said.

"The social concepts of Christianity rest, of course, upon this principle of the Incarnation," and that in serving the secular and worldly life of our neighbors we are, "serving the incarnate life of God, and that the secular and worldly life is also consecrated, dedicated, given to God. I never hear the words of the great eucharist—and I hear them often—that here we present ourselves, our souls and bodies, to be a living sacrifice—I never hear them without realizing that what we are presenting is ourselves, our problems, our temptations. But not mine alone, not my little petty human, mean temptations, but the temptations, the problems of all mankind. So, we have that great comfort and consolation of being able, week after week, day after day, to present ourselves, our souls and bodies and all our temptation in the great eucharistic sacrifice to God himself."

Stressing her point that the special vocation of the laity is the political, economic, cultural, and social life of community, she said, "the laity might have some responsibility with regard to education, with regard to the terrific defects of modern education; and that the Christian laity perhaps have now a new obligation to analyze and find what are the reasons why we have no educated people, no people sufficiently educated to assume the responsibilities which modern life demands of them.

"Some of you have read, I am sure, this book of Lecomte du Noüy, *Human Destiny*. A great physical scientist, a man who was a specialist on atomic energy, nuclear physics, and who writes to the effect that [quoting from the book] 'The whole world realizes the advantage which would result from the fact that the great majority of men could be trusted. There is a unanimity of thought in this which is to be found nowhere else except on the subject of the Ten Commandments, but the effort made to impress the idea indelibly on the minds of children in the shape of automatic conditioned reflexes is so slight, that one is aghast.'[59] In other words, he goes on to say that there is no one today who can be trusted. Men have come to the point where they do not trust each other. He, as a nuclear physicist, says, 'We nuclear physicists have discovered a great power, a great and terrific power, which we do not dare to entrust to men because they cannot be trusted.'[60] I wish everybody would read it, particularly the last two chapters."

According to Perkins, Lecomte argued that, through our educational processes, we have, blotted out that moral responsibility which is the chief purpose of education. If we cannot build up people who can be trusted, she said, "how can we develop a society which can be called a good society, a society which can be called a Christian social order? Or how can we build up that relationship to God…which is essential not only to the whole society, but essential to us as individuals?"

Developing a Christian Attitude

She asserted that in addition to conducting the affairs of the world according to Christian principles, Christians must also establish for themselves the Christian attitude and the Christian point of view. She said Christians not only participate in the life of the community through liturgical worship, "but they participate in it—particularly we, the laity do—in the responsibility which we assume and which we accept for conducting the world's affairs." Because hardly anyone refuses, she said, "to accept the responsibility of a job, we will say, in public office, a job as the head of a great bank, a job as the head of a great educational institution, a job as the head of a great industry…but how do they know they can discharge those responsibilities morally? That is one of the things that we who are laity and those who represent the whole church—the bishops, the clergy, and the laity—have to answer to those who have accepted the responsibility" of conducting the secular affairs of humankind.

"I think myself that we of the church have a tremendous advantage in our insight into the problem because of the fact that we are not unaware of the contribution and of the responsibility that we of the laity have in the worship of the church—the liturgical worship of the church. We know that the offering of the holy sacrifice in the eucharist is not complete without our offering, too. And, as we know that, we are able to accept for ourselves…this great obligation to offer the work that we do in the world…as a part of the obligation which is that due and proper sacrifice of all…in the face of the glory of God."

Noting that she had previously touched on the concept of a "superior allegiance" owed to the laws of God (see Chapter Two), she said people must develop a "detailed harmony" between their conduct of secular affairs and "the laws of God." She said we must recognize that the law of God is dominant and must be dominant and that all people, "whether they are in public life and in public office, or whether they are in the various professions, must first admit and first concern themselves with the laws of God." And that no one, "whether he be doctor or lawyer or merchant or manufacturer or laborer or public official, can think of himself as carrying out the full obligations of his job, of his responsibility, merely because he is efficient and competent and obeys the laws of the land and doesn't defy the ethical concepts of his profession. He can never really adjust himself and account for himself unless he also first bows to the laws of God."

She reiterated her assertion that the chief end of humanity is "to know, to love, and to serve God and finally, to be joined with him in eternity…," adding, "Now, this is not a private affair. This is an affair which involves all the people of God; and none of us can deny it, and none of us dares to deny it—to know, to love, to serve God, and finally, to be joined with him. We have discussed that as a part of the understanding with which we people of 1948 regard our social responsibilities and regard the good life and the good social order. The recognition that the chief purpose of Man is not only to glorify God, but finally to be joined with him, to move toward God; and that we must do those things which will help our fellow men to move toward God.

"We have raised the question, too, of Man's duty, even his obligation under God, to accept himself as he is and to be reconciled to himself within God's love. This, I think, is one of the hardest and most complicated things for us modern Christians to understand. We have discussed it a little bit, but even if we are to love our fellow men—and the law of God tells us to love our fellow men as we love ourselves—we must recognize that God loves us, you and me—we individuals, as uncouth, so unworthy, so irregular, so inadequate, so without ability, really."

Others are just like us, she said, and if we are to love them as we love ourselves, "then suddenly we are faced not with the idea that we must love ourselves in a selfish way, but that we must understand ourselves. That we must explain ourselves. That we must accept ourselves and be reconciled to ourselves with those talents, with those handicaps which God gave us. That we must somehow or other find the way to move toward God to our own destined end as we accept the idea and the responsibility of moving our fellow men toward God. We move our fellow men, or at least we have in recent years thought we could move our fellow men toward God by providing, you know, for a Christian order of society, a method of living where we could have good houses, houses in which Christian families could grow up, and reasonable wages so that men could provide for their own families and carry on that family life and constructive program which is so essential. We have thought in terms of the living God incarnate represented in the lives of the common, ordinary people of the community. But who are we but the common, ordinary people of the community? And is it not true that God also loves us? He loves the working man down the street. He loves us, too, and modern man's confusion and modern man's problem is to find the way by which he himself can associate himself with the social needs of Man, with mankind as a whole, and still find this redeeming quality of the union of Man with God in his spiritual life."

She said modern humanity's greatest obligation is "to raise up and educate a society which understands the meaning of the life of God incarnate in human affairs. But primarily if we are to recognize that the purpose of God [is that we] should move toward God and toward this great destiny of union with God, then we must accept the responsibility of each man and each woman in our human society to move himself toward God.

"For that we are ill-equipped, and we know we are. We are distraught. We are confused. And we are grateful to the church for such guidance as the church gives us in moving toward the realization of the union of Man with God. We say "the union of Man with God"—we spell Man with a capital letter—but we say, '"Man" includes me, oh Lord,' and I, too, must share in that great redemption which is represented by the Incarnation, the Incarnation of God in the form of Man, with the nature of Man, carrying in his own person all the burdens, all the sins, all the confusions, all the problems not only of the men of the day,...but the problems of men as of this day, the problems of men unto eternity," she said.

The Mind of Christ

"So, our knowledge of God and of his redemption becomes a problem in having within ourselves those gifts of the Incarnation which we call the mind of Christ, and finding for ourselves as individuals and as a community what is the mind of Christ. Now, a good life, of course, is very easy for us, and most of us would like to fall back on this, I know. But it is not enough for those who have thought about it. We would like to fall back upon a good humanitarian policy, a good humanitarian life. We would like to say, 'Oh, Lord, thou knowest that I have given to the poor. I have visited the sick. I have visited those in prison. I have done all works of good works, oh, Lord!' But we know in the days of this later revelation that that is not enough.

"We know that humanitarianism is not enough. And I say this as one who has given a life to humanitarian activities. They are essential. They must be done. They are a part of the service that Man owes to God and owes to his fellow men. But they are not enough because God also made you and me for himself, and we must move ourselves toward God and toward that union with God, which is the primary destiny of all men, and which is the reason and the purpose for all these acts which may in themselves be good but which serve mankind and serve God only because they move other men toward God himself."

Turning to the question of how people can actually move themselves toward God, she said, "Well, you know as well as I do, and the clergy tried to tell us so often. And we are so perverse and so confused and so settled upon our own ways of doing things that we don't always take it in. But somehow or other I think we have come in recent years to understand that a teaching clergy and a teaching church can show thousands and hundreds of thousands and millions of our co-religionists and of other Christian people how to find the way by which they, too, may approach that union with God which is the chief end of Man, which is the real purpose of Man on earth." She said there were only a few people "in our part of the church who are trying to learn and determined to learn how to approach that union with God...." She said they had worked out a few "of the principles by which we can learn how to be united with God, how to take part in this mysterious act of Incarnation in which God gave himself to men for their uplifting. Primarily we must and we can and we know how to practice the presence of God. Now *that*, I think, is not ordinarily regarded as part of the social obligation of mankind, for if we would build a Christian social order we must practice the presence of God; and for ourselves as individuals we must also practice the presence of God.

"I don't know of any better book on the subject than that little bit of a volume—so few letters, so few interviews, just a few printed words—of Brother Lawrence which he called *The Practice of the Presence of God.* He was a very commonplace person, so he says. He had to wash dishes and cook in the monastery, and occasionally he had to go down to the south of France to buy wine, which he was no judge of and didn't know how to do. He had to do always the things he didn't know how to do. These were things that were given him to do. He didn't know how to do them, but he practiced the presence of God, and he found and discovered for himself and for others...that if you know the presence of God you are always able to do those things which God requires of you.

"Isn't that, after all, what we have to do for ourselves? Don't we have to educate ourselves? Isn't that what the good life means for the individual in our community? We must educate ourselves to be like Brother Lawrence. We must educate ourselves to bear those burdens and responsibilities which we have to bear. We must train and educate ourselves to understand what the principles of the presence of God are. We have to educate ourselves almost as we would educate a young person who was under us in a professional and economic capacity. We would understand that he was a young man. He didn't know and we would expect to train him and explain to him and give him opportunity to exercise his judgment and exercise his understanding and to analyze his problem....We have to take ourselves as a young and inexperienced person, young certainly in the spiritual laws and in the spiritual nature of our relationship to God. We don't know. We are inexperienced. We have to find out. We are trying, and we have to educate ourselves.

"So, first of all, we have to think of ourselves as we are. We have to make an estimate of the situation. We have to understand what it is that we are aiming at. What is our goal? Certainly, our goal is the goal that is revealed to us in the Incarnation. Just as it is revealed to us as a social obligation, so it is revealed to us as an individual obligation to understand the Incarnation of our Lord, to understand that he is here and now, without time or space, without the limitations of time or space, that he is available to us for strength, that he is available to us as a pattern and as a reason for performing our duties and our obligations in a way which is in the mind of Christ.

"I often wondered if it wouldn't be good for us to think back and recognize that Christ is King, and accept for ourselves the conception that Christ is King of this world, and to act and behave as though Christ were present and ruling. It would make a great difference in the things we do from day to day if we recognized, if we said to ourselves, 'Well, Christ is King. What does Christ require of us in this situation and in this relationship? What is it that is obligatory upon me because Christ is King. I have no choice. The ruler of this universe requires this, and this, and this!'

"But most of us, although we give lip service to the idea that Christ is King, do not examine our consciences from that point of view. And then, of course, those who must somehow or other educate themselves, train themselves as any child would be trained, as any young professional person would be trained in an office or a manufacturing establishment, do not always realize the value and importance of the spiritual exercise as a method of training.

"This is one of the things which I think today more than ever we have to accept—the discipline of an exercise. The

Quakers always intrigued me because, although they have not followed with us all of the conception of the purpose and function and divine establishment of the church itself, they have, nevertheless out of their own experience of the inner light, been able to conceive of a disciplinary practice which would bring them as individuals into harmony with the will of God. I think we can learn so much from people like that, people who, although they do not agree with us at every point, nevertheless have, out of their own experience, so much to give that we cannot afford to avoid it.

"I think we must study that whole question of spiritual exercise and, in particular, we must study that form of the spiritual exercise—if we would make progress toward union with God—which helps us to examine our own inadequacies and helps us to examine the reasons why we are separated from God and why we are not actually united with God and performing in such a way as to unite us to the will of God. Because we want to be united to the will of God.

"Now, what do we do? What would you do with a young person whom you were training in your office or in your business or in your trade or profession? You would sit down with him and you would make an examination of the situation. You would make an examination and an estimate of the situation. You know, every military commander makes an estimate of the situation before he either goes into battle or before he makes any plans. And what does he do? He evaluates all the factors here, all the factors there. What does the Christian do? The Christian evaluates the strength, if I may say so, of Satan, the strength of the devil, and he evaluates his own strength and his own weakness, and by true and honest self-examination he finds out what his own weakness is.

Social Conscience and Its Examination

"Now, I think that really, for the progress of the individual and the progress of the society, of the community in a Christian way of life, that the most important thing we have to do—and I mean this with regard to Christians in New York in the year 1948—is to make an examination of conscience both for the individual and for the society, and an estimate of the situation based upon that examination of conscience. I know that the examination of conscience is not a popular spiritual exercise, but I think that it is essential if men are to understand themselves and to understand their shortcomings, and therefore to clear out the mess and the debris and to make progress toward union with God.... Whether or not one feels that auricular confession to a priest is essential is not important. The examination of conscience will bring to light those items, those conceptions, those actions and those ideas which hold the human being back from the true union with God, hold him back from the love of

God, hold him back from the love of his neighbors, hold him back from the perfect conformation to the laws of God which he desires to achieve.

"Now, I do not think it is difficult. I do not think it is impossible for the ordinary man to make a true examination of conscience. It certainly will be varied with different people. It will be varied according to their life experience. It will be varied according to their understanding of what sin is. But sin is always nothing in the world except separation from God. Anything that separates a man from God is sinful. He doesn't need any other criteria of judgment. It isn't a puritanical rule of this or that behavior. It is those things which separate him from God, which prevent him from seeing and understanding the true nature of God, and prevent him from uniting his life with the life of God." She added that practice, experience, and persistence make it possible for a people to analyze themselves.

"Modern psychology has taught us a lot of things. It has showed up to all of us certain weaknesses in our defenses, certain weaknesses not only in Christian practices, certain weaknesses in our own understanding of the purposes of mankind. Because that is the case, it is helpful, and I think for myself and perhaps for many others, important that people should examine their consciences against a standard pattern—you know, generally accepted rules of behavior like the Ten Commandments, or the seven deadly sins.

"Well, now, I know that an advanced soul would push those out with, 'That's very primitive!' I know it is very simple and primitive, but for most of us to examine ourselves against the pattern of the Ten Commandments, or by the pattern of the seven deadly sins, is an important experience; and most of us never get through with it. We get bogged down and upset and confused and say, 'Oh, my God, I am a sinner!'—long before we get through with the recital of the seven deadly sins. I think it is important because most of us are so ignorant about moral values and moral qualities—it is important that we do follow a manual.

"I used to think that was very silly myself. You know, I thought—well, it is an aspect of the sin of pride, I suppose, that one certainly has a better evaluation of one's idiosyncrasies and one's departure from the standard rule than could possibly be indicated by a rule of life or by a manual of examination. But the interesting thing is that the more we know about human nature and the more we know about our fellow human beings, the more we realize that other people don't see their faults. You know that. How well we all know it! The others don't see their faults. How is it that I am able to see my faults if others don't see theirs?

"So, I think that perhaps to examine myself by a pattern, by a manual, which those who have seen the faults of many have devised, is a help to me to distinguish between the various forms of pride, the various aspects in which the sin of pride can demonstrate itself.

"So, I say that if we are to have a good life in the community, a good life of individuals, a good life of the society, a revival of the community, we must expect that there will be an examination of conscience both of the individual and of the community. And in applying the examination of conscience, the question of what is right and wrong, what has this society, what has this country done, what has this city done, what has this community done, what has this parish done that is wrong and against the will of God, which holds us back from union with Almighty God...?" In using such a pattern, she said, "we will have a much greater understanding of each other and of each other's temptations. Then as I see the problems of the individual in trying to be a part of a good community, a Christian community, I am more and more aware of the fact that there must be for those of us who hope to contribute to a Christian community, a rule of life, so simple, that we can rest on it when we are tired and confused and unable to think intellectually, or to experience spiritually those highest values. A rule of life, a rule of prayer, a rule of concentrations, a rule of reception of the sacraments, a rule of understanding. Is that impossible?" she asked her audience.

"I, myself, think that every Christian person should never fail to remind himself daily in an act of faith, in an act of hope, in an act of love, and an act of contrition, of what his great purpose in life is. It may be very brief; it may be very simple. I wish and I hope that we can develop for the community, as well as for the individual, a sense of the principle of reparation, of the making good for those things which we have done which are wrong, which are offensive to Almighty God, which have damaged the fabric of society, which have hurt the hope and aspiration of other individuals with whom we deal. There is an enormous area of understanding within that pattern of aspiration which can find its outlet in an act of reparation," she said.

"So, as we come forward now to the conception of the spiritual exercise out of which the individuals who make up the Christian community can develop their own souls—can advance their own progress toward God—we raise also the question of the Christian community. For I do not think myself that we can establish a Christian order of society, and I know in this that there are many doctors of the church and several learned men, notably Mr. T.S. Eliot, in recent years, who say that a Christian order of society is not dependent upon any considerable number of Christians in the world. But I do not think we can greatly advance the Christian order of society, at least not in the United States of America for which we have responsibility, and we have no responsibility or little responsibility elsewhere, unless we can do it here."

Advancing the Christian Life

"I think we cannot advance the Christian order of society unless we can advance our own Christian life; and our Christian life, as we have said over and over again in these discussions, is not a matter of behaving in a good and kind and charitable way. Certainly, without charity Man is nothing, and charity is the first law of God. But the great and eternal purpose of mankind is to advance toward union with God; and if he has union with God, if he has a sense of union with God, he will then inevitably, because he knows God, choose those patterns of behavior which make for the welfare and ennoblement and enhancement and advance of his fellow human beings toward a knowledge of God and toward union with God."

Without such knowledge, she said, people "cannot find their way as individuals, and the revival of community is, I think, dependent not upon every human being having a Christian mystical experience of union with God; but a Christian community is dependent upon there being in a very large area of our society a recognition of, and an appreciation of, the chief end of Man, and of the accomplishments of thousands and hundreds of thousands of individuals of that great end of a spiritual union with God. These are confused sayings, I know, but not to you who are members of the faith; not to you who have the great sacramental principles given to you, preserved for you, handed down to you by the church. Not to you who have in your original teaching as children, and in your daily and regular experience of the life of the church, the opportunity for union with God through the sacraments. However weak and feeble and small and inadequate that sense of union may be, nevertheless it is a pre-vision of what the great union of all mankind with God and his purposes can be.

"So, I feel that the Christian order of society requires not only a pattern of social cooperation and of social justice which can be expressed in law, in politics, in economics, in social and cultural relations, but requires also a corps of individuals who have themselves experienced, and who will work and struggle and even fight to provide for themselves, and for those who are dependent upon them spiritually, that relationship of the union with God.

"So, when we think of the revival of community in American life, and community has almost passed out as an idea; we have substituted the state; we have substituted law; we have substituted all sorts of things for community—but community means people of common purpose, people of common spiritual experience, people of common idealism. We must, I think, re-establish that community. We must establish it in terms of service. We can establish it certainly in terms of ideas. We can express it in terms of ideas; but we must also express it in terms of service.

"I think that in these days when the state tends to be too large, and I as one of those who has promoted the services which the state can render to individuals, recognize the hazard that the state can [become] too important unless it is constantly integrated, constantly infiltrated with the Christian concept of Christian service with a community. So that when we see a social security law giving old age benefits to John Jones and Mary Smith, we are able to associate ourselves with that program and that system in such a way that we know that Christian people in a Christian community are taking care of the needs of the aged.... I have always hoped that out of the sense of Christian community there would come those old cooperative enterprises which used to be in smaller and simpler societies non-commercial, simple, helpful, where women of the community went in to care for the sick and the dying. I always remember that in my town when anybody was really very, very ill and wasn't going to live, that old Doctor Stetson used to say, 'I think you had better send for Suzy Fosset!'

"Suzy Fosset was the good Christian woman who came when there wasn't any more hope that the old man or the old lady could live. But Suzy would come in and with a Christian grace would not only ease the pain and confusion and worry of dying, but would reconcile the family to the fact that death was, and that death is, a part of Christian life and Christian conception. I have always hoped that the time might come back when the brethren would put the coffin up on their shoulders and bury the old man, the member of our society, the friend of our youth; and when it was all done in the terms of Christian service of the community, one to the other. When even—and I hate to say this in these days—but when you and I and others went out to do a little practical nursing in our own parish, you know, for those who didn't have the $10 a day necessary to employ a practical nurse; but when you and I and others went out and changed the bed and bathed the patient and gave her medication.

"For most sick people, there is no very scientific routine of nursing. I know that. I have given all sorts of treatments, and I know that anybody can do it, a little awkwardly perhaps, but anybody can do it. Any good honest woman, and I guess a man, if necessary, could do it," she said, invoking laughter from the audience.

"In the army they did it. They didn't have enough medical men and medical corps men to do it. As a matter of fact, in my town a young medical corps man who had no experience at all made a diagnosis of a ruptured intestine that saved the life of an individual who had been brought in and operated badly for just little minor appendix.

"All kinds of ignorant and simple people can be trained, you know. During the war, we trained medical attendants—whatever they call them—practical nurses. It can be done.

"What about the care of young children? These are Christian things that you have to do with the laws of God. I wouldn't interfere with anybody's way of making a living, but the care of young children and the care of the sick and the burial of the dead, and the care of the aged and the support of the family—all these things have to do, do they not, with the laws of God. These have to with the will of God on earth for his family, for his people, for his friends, for those for whom he has died.

A Community of Common Purpose

"So, why can we not, as we think in terms of law and order and legislation and all that sort of thing, establish a Christian principle of a social order which shall express in its sense of justice, its sense of the worth, the dignity of each man because God made him. Christ died for him, and it is our duty, therefore, to support and help him. Why cannot we, in that kind of Christian order, also develop a Christian community, a community of common purpose, of common hope, of common recognition of the source of our salvation?"

Calling for a common recognition of God's purposes humankind and a common recognition of the meaning of the Incarnation of God living in the form of humanity today, eternally with us, she went on to say, "The only hope we have, the only source of strength we have to do any of these things, either as individuals or as a community or as an organized society is, of course, the fact that God is with us, promising his holy spirit to help those who would work with him. He has given us the strength. Now, we deny it all the time, but we know it, and there are hundreds of thousands, millions, who testify that in times of great trouble, in times of terrific stress, in times when they were not adequate to do what they had to do, our Lord stood beside them, and they knew it.

"These are [sic] the personal experience—a mystical experience you may say—but a true experience which indicates not only that in a Christian order of society...[but also] with the Christian struggling in the world today in 1948, these mystical experiences are still possible. But that the strength that results from them enables Man to work with God for the accomplishment of that which he would desire not only for society, but for the redemption of each individual, including me, as well as this great order of mankind to whom we are so well disposed, but whose relationship to us in their struggles we so often forget."

With that last plea, she concluded her formal remarks to a round of applause from the audience and then took questions from the floor.

"Now, the Committee of St. Bede, for which I have great respect and which, by the way, I meant to mention as one of the methods by which Christian individuals can do their duty, or a part of their duty in society, by offering the means of education to those who want to know and want to find out what the experience of the saints has been—the Committee of St. Bede's tells me that I ought to answer a few questions. I'd be glad to do it if I know the answers."

The first questioner asked, "Could you say something about religious education in public schools?"

Perkins responded, "Well, as for me, I think that the dropping of religious education out of the public schools was one of the most devastating and unfortunate things that ever happened to this country. When I was a child I went to a public school for two years and there wasn't any question at all about religious education there. I mean, everybody knew that God was, and that we were here to worship him. We said the prayers. They read the psalms. They read the New Testament and the Old Testament, and we sang hymns, and we had a little bit of religious education. As a matter of fact, the education was not profoundly secular.

"I think myself that it is extremely important that we establish some way by which Christian children can be given religious education, and I do not believe that it is divisive. I know that our Jewish friends say to me that the reason they oppose it is that they think it is divisive; that it divides the Christians from the Jews and that it separates people and it gives them false ideas that they are not all one people. I so truly believe that individuals who are trained in the Christian faith cannot have feelings of bitterness or opposition to Jews. They know that all men are created by God and that God has revealed himself in many ways, and they are grateful to the Jewish people and to the Jewish religion for the preservation and handling down of that knowledge of God which was undoubtedly revealed to the Hebrew people.

"So, I feel that our Jewish friends are mistaken when they feel that it would separate the Christians from the Jews. I think it is extraordinarily important that in every community where any of our Christians have a voice, we should re-establish the practice and the habit of the training and education and informing of children about the principles of the Christian faith. That is in the public schools. Of course, in the church schools and in the private schools, if I may say so, I think it is even more important because there has been a habit in recent years, you know, of treating it all as though it were just one of those pleasant cultural devices, and that you wouldn't want your children to be ignorant of the cultural values and cultural basis of the Christian religion.

"You'd want them to know the great books of religion, but it didn't mean anything to them. It was no challenge to them. I don't believe that children can grow up to be moral and intelligent and make those intelligent moral choices that must be made except with the sense of their own divine destiny, and that they have to answer finally to God Almighty. If they think of Christ as King and reigning and their necessity to answer to him, they will not make too many evil and wrong choices."

Someone from the audience then asked, "What is your cure for unemployment and depression?"

"This is really an intelligent person," she said, "because he adds, 'This is the $64 question.'

"Well, I don't think that anybody can answer that question authoritatively and completely. One of the things, you see, that is the matter with secular society today, and the society where the intellectual concepts about economics and social policy derive from Marx rather than Christ, is that people are always trying to give you a theoretical pattern. 'You can do this, this, and that, and everything will be all right.' That is not so...but there are many small things which can be done...

"I have to go into this because I wrote a chapter about this in the little book which the bishops published at the close of the

General Convention, called *Christianity Takes a Stand*. I hate to say this. There may be a bishop here. But the House of Bishops apparently didn't want to take the responsibility for some of the secular things," she teased, drawing laughter from the audience. "So, they asked a lot of laymen to write little pieces about one thing and another, about race relations, and about social problems, and about unemployment, and about a few other things. Then they gave it their blessing in the beginning chapter and the ending chapter. But anyhow they asked me to write a little piece about unemployment and how to prevent it, and I did. I did the very best I could.

She drew more laughter as she said, "I don't like to push the book, but it sells for only cents, and the church doesn't get any royalties, and I don't either. But at any rate, I did do my best there to point out that while there is no known cure for these depressions, there are a number of small (some of them not so small) things which can be done, which tend to mitigate the effects of the economic cycle, and tend to maintain employment and maintain the economic activities of life during periods when normal demands of the market fall off.

"I pointed out, among other things, the utilization, either by the state or by the community, of the technique of the remission of taxes on those enterprises which would employ large numbers of people, and the technique by which individual employers could plan their production in such a way as to make it possible for them to guarantee a certain number of weeks of employment per year. I mean really fifty-two weeks of work per year. There are a large number of employers who do this already, and it could be done in many others, although not all of them. There is no moral obliquity attaching to an industry which can't do it because it has either a high seasonal turnover or doesn't make the kind of goods that can be stored.

"I went into a number of those things and pointed out particularly that the utilization of public works as a technique of preventing the disaster—not unemployment or not depression, itself—but the individual disaster of no wages and no work for a period of depression, was a technique which could be used by the state under Christian conscience. That it *should* be used by the state under Christian conscience, and that it should be put into operation *early* in the depression, not late. To do it early could make it a very effective technique."

"And I went into quite a learned discussion—I like to point it out to you because my principal economic adviser wrote that part of it" she said, again drawing laughter, "—about taxation, and how it could be handled and manipulated in such a way as to tend to mitigate the decline of an economy, and therefore to prevent unemployment.

"I think that all these things can be done with a Christian conscience and by the cooperation of the Christian employer with a community, with a state which is influenced by (perhaps dominated by, I hope dominated by) Christian conscience. The part of Christians in all this is to see that the state does care about what happens to the individual and doesn't say—"Oh, well, it can't be helped."

Auricular Confession

Another participant asked, "If auricular confession [private confession to a priest] is not essential, what better way is there to be relieved of the burden of sin?"

Perkins responded, "Well, I don't know of any better way, but I know that there are many people—and our church does not require auricular confession—who feel that they receive the same absolution and the same relief of their burden of sin by making their own confession to Almighty God in the form of a detailed, specific confession based upon their examination of conscience.

"I would be willing always to go along with that because the important thing really is that a man should measure himself, and should know those items in which he has failed to conform to the laws of God, and in which he has failed to conform to his own highest promptings in his moral and spiritual life. If he can satisfy his conscience by the provision in the general confession which our church provides, and if he can satisfy his conscience even by the further consideration of the confession which our church provides for those who are sick and perhaps dying, then I think he is justified in doing that.

"I would not for one moment, because I have found auricular confession to be a help and to be a great illumination and a great exercise in humility, which is the greatest of the virtues and the hardest to acquire—I would not for one moment say, since our church does not require it, that another man must follow the same procedure. But I do say that no man or no woman can possibly understand the situation in which he stands with relation to those sins which separate him from God unless he makes a periodic and rather regular examination of his conscience to see in what detailed particulars he has done those things which he ought not to have done and left undone those things which he ought to have done.

"It is so easy to say those general words. It is so hard to bring oneself to say, 'Yes, I should have gone to see old cousin Suzy. She is sick. She is old. She is disagreeable. She needs me.' I mean, those are the things we don't do until we are pressed by some examination of conscience which brings us down to the realities.

"I think that for adult people, as for children, that those things are important in the education of the spirit and the education of the mentality of human beings to make them realize what it is that separates them from God. How can they hope to go on to that union with God if they do not understand, do not even admit, and in their pride even deny?

"I know a man who I once laughingly said, 'Now, John, you know what is the matter with you? This is just nothing but the sin of pride!' And he drew himself up and said, 'Yes. I have my pride. I am as proud as anybody else.'

"There are many, many people, and I dare say among us, who think the sin of pride is a virtue and do not realize the extent to which it is the hardest thing in the world for modern, adult, intellectual people to understand. You know that St. Augustine said, and I have so many times gained great wisdom and virtue and help from this—that the great sin of the intellectuals, of all intellectual people, was the sin of pride. That all people who had a good mind were likely to be tempted by the sin of pride; and that the only way to overcome it was by the virtue of love. And St. Augustine said, and he wrote it down, that when he was in the midst of his most terrific intellectual activities, out of which he must have had great satisfaction (we all do out of our intellectual activities)—he said, 'Nine times a day I make an act of love. My God, I love thee above all others, and for thy sake I love my neighbors as myself.'

"You know, in times of stress and temptation I, myself, have found that a pattern that should be followed is to say it every morning, every noon, every night—'My God, I love thee above all others, and for thy sake I love my neighbors as myself.'

"I don't think that we know a great deal about modern psychology. Perhaps we are 'psychologizing' ourselves, as they say, but why not? This is the way we wish to be. We want to love, do we not? We want to love God. We desire to love God. God gave himself for us. We desire to meet him in love, and we must use every device and every technique we know to keep ourselves from departing from that pattern of love. And if the constant repetition of that conception, 'My God, I love thee…'—is a help, than I think we must do it. I always remember St. Augustine, a great and learned man, a worldly man, a man knowing the world as all the rest of us know the world, and yet giving himself to God, who found that pattern essential to keeping him on an even keel."

Another person asked, "Doesn't early training have a lot to do with the intuition? It is God given."

"Yes, I think it does," Perkins said. "I am glad somebody asked that question because I think that we do not sufficiently appreciate or respect that intuitive quality of the human mind, which we all recognize and which we mistrust somehow when it comes into play in religion. But the intuitive quality of the human mind is one of the most important and significant aspects of mentality. Even Aristotle and Plato recognized it as the basis of the human mentality. And you know, that insight, which is closely related to it, is essential to a man's sanity. If any of you ever had any experience at all with people who are mentally ill, you have known that the doctors said to you, 'I'm sorry. I'm afraid we can't do much for him. He has no insight.' Or the doctor says, 'Yes, he will get well. He has good insight.'

"Insight and intuition are the same things—this understanding of the inner nature of the being. Insight and intuition are essential for a normal healthy mind, and yet you find people who will say that you should not follow intuition. You must! Logic is deceptive. Logic is a tool. Logic is something to be used if it will help you to find the answers but is not an essential to a mental comprehension, to an intellectual and spiritual comprehension of the problem.

"While I agree that early training has a lot to do with the development of intuition, I know, too, that it is God given. But is it not our duty as Christians to help children and young people and adults, too, whom we know, to develop that quality of intuition which enables them to apprehend the idea of God? Is it not essential that we should give them in early training, or even in adult training, a better conception of that?

"Of course, I think one can never say often enough that the church has not sufficiently provided for the education of adults. Although I happen to have been so fortunate as to live in two parishes—one here and one in Washington—where the education of adults is certainly a part of the burden of the clergy, and they do it remarkably well, I know that throughout the church generally there is not sufficient attention to the actual education of the laity, the adult laity.

"Many grown people who have been confirmed do not know the principle of the Incarnation, the principle of the Redemption. They do not know and understand what those principles are, or how they apply to themselves. Much less do they understand the principle of Christian ethics, which derive from the Incarnation and the Redemption and the laws of God."

The Christendom Group

A request for more information about the Christendom group, which she had mentioned previously was the next question directed to Perkins.

"The Christendom group," she said, "is a group in England which has been associated around a quarterly magazine called *Christendom*, which was, of course, suspended or greatly reduced in size during the war and which is now, I think, by way of being revived." She described the group of "devout, catholic, praying people who have a great concern, as the Quakers would say, for the social mission of the church, and who, seeing in their own lives and in their own circumstances certain very problematical situations, have, for the most part, thrown their personal lives into the problems of the poor.

"Some of you may now—you may have seen the houses in London that are called Basil Jellico houses. Basil Jellico was a young priest of the church who saw the depraved and terrible housing, and he utilized his influence and his priesthood and his leadership to persuade the members of his parish and of adjoining parishes, and finally of the Bishop of London, to put money into the building of good houses, good multiple dwellings for Christian people, long before the London County Council had thought of these new modern houses.

"To this day the Basil Jellico houses are more human; you'd rather live there, you see, than you would in one of the London County Council houses, although they are all about the same as regards drainage and heating and all that kind of thing. There is air. There is an atmosphere. There is a friendliness. There is a sense of Christian community about them which is essential, and which is what Father Jellico tried to contribute to that idea.

"Now, the Christendom group has been a group of people that conducted in the city for many, many years, a house, a great general gathering place—a flophouse, if you want to say—for unemployed and homeless menials in the name of Christ, always with the clear understanding that 'We do this for you, my brother, because we love Jesus and we hope you do'—evangelical, if you wish— but people of our church, of our faith, of our communion, who had a great sense of the social problems and the social obligations.

"Now, for the last thirty years they have been conducting a summer school of Christian sociology, as they call it, at which I have had the privilege to be in attendance on at least two occasions. Canon [V.A.] Demant who was here last winter, some of you heard him—he is a Canon of the Cathedral of St. Paul and was here, I think, in residence at Berkeley Theological Seminary for several months and who lectured in several places—is one of the prime movers in the Christendom group. He is a man, very learned in theology, but very warm-hearted and very understanding of the social problems of the life of the people who live around St. Paul's Cathedral....

"The Bishop of London, whose official seat is in St. Paul's Cathedral—as you know, there is almost no parish there, a lot of impoverished people living on the outskirts of it—called Canon Demant, I think from somewhere in Yorkshire, to come and reside in the cathedral precincts, and sort of to canvass and build up a Christian community around the cathedral. Between them they are having a great influence upon the conception of the

English church, or what the obligation is to the people of London, the life and labors of the people of London.

"Tawney [economic historian R.H. Tawney], who many of you know, is a part of that Christendom group. Maurice Reckitt, Basil Basingstote are members of that group. T.S. Eliot. Dorothy Sayers. People who have an intellectual understanding of the Christian faith and of the Catholic religion, who also understand and are particularly touched by the social implications of it, are prime movers in this group. It has been going on a long time and it is, in no sense, a separatist group. It is just a group of intellectuals who, within the church, very, very loyal to the church, are trying to emphasize this idea that Christendom means the social, as well as the individual, salvation of all mankind. That Christ died for mankind, for all men, and that all of them have equal value in the eyes of God."

"May a Boston Unitarian ask a question?" one person asked, to which Perkins responded, "Why, certainly, right up my alley. I am a New Englander, myself."

"Instead of wishing to create a Christian society," the questioner asked, "why not say a 'decent' society, recognizing the noble aspiration of the Hebrew prophets and of those like Gandhi who belong to quite alien faiths."

"I agree that one should speak of a 'decent' society," Perkins said, "and I think that in an earlier conference here I did say that on this time of a good society and of a decent order of society, that here was the place where people of all kinds of faiths who believe in God could cooperate.

"Now, I would not myself have much faith—and perhaps I'm wrong and narrow-minded about this—I would not invest my money or my person in a project for the improvement of society which did not have within it, as its leaders and principals, people who believed in God. Now, I will not say in what aspect of God they know him, because God reveals himself in many ways. But the only people in my experience—and I may be wrong and narrow-minded about it—who will stick when things are hard and tough and the going is pretty difficult, are those who believe in God and know they have got to answer, and who intend to answer to God Almighty, for what they do in the creation of a decent order of society.

Answering to God

"I always remember a labor leader, not a Christian himself, who said to me when he had agreed that I should appoint an arbitrator in an industrial dispute he was having with the employers of his union—'Whom are you going to appoint?' I said, 'Well, you know, you are not supposed to ask me that question.' 'Well,' he said, 'I don't want to know the name of the person, but I would like to know something about him.' I was intrigued and I said, 'Well, now, what do you want to know about him?' 'Well,' he said, 'you know arbitration is very tricky. I would like to be sure that the person who was the arbitrator believes in God, and that he has some kind of religion, that he believes he has got to answer to God for what he does. Because this has to do with the lives and the welfare of my people, and if he has only got to answer to you and to the President and to the Congress, well, that is not enough. I want somebody who will perform with a conscience, who knows that he has got to answer to God.'

"I always remembered that because it is really a very important distinction between those who are merely humanistic in their attitudes, and those who know that, whether they be Hebrews or Unitarians or any of the other categories of believers, they believe in Almighty God and in the end that Man must answer to God, and that their consciences will answer to God. And I believe we should.

"I think that at this point in the creating and establishing of an order of Christian society, here is a point where there can be full cooperation. Now, we of the church—and this is a group of church people—have a particular responsibility, so we feel and I do think truthfully, because we have had handed down to us by our bishops and our priests in the apostolic order of succession a faith which we do not doubt, and which we cannot doubt, and which we are obligated to believe, which tells us of the true nature of God, the true nature of Man, and of Man's relationship to God."

She continued, saying it is a faith which "informs our conscience and stimulates our hope and desire to do the will of God, and which beyond that has preserved within itself the opportunity and the duty to give to us those sacramental gifts, from which we are enabled to associate ourselves, as unworthy as we are, with God and his principles; and to understand through that sacrament of the holy eucharist—to understand, limited as we are—something of what the purposes of Almighty God are for men, have the strength which we can have through that to perform our part of the securing of those purposes.

"That's why we have a special mission which we cannot ignore—however much we may desire—to cooperate will all others to bring about a decent order of society." She concluded her remarks to another round of applause.

Top: St. John's, Ithaca, where Perkins worshiped while teaching at Cornell. *Bottom*: St. Andrew's, Newcastle, her summer parish near the family homestead in Maine.

Chapter Five

"Be Ye Steadfast"

Christian tradition holds that Christ alone is perfect. Saints are not. Saints are fully human beings in whom the light of Christ burned so brightly during their earthly ministries that we are confident they are in heaven, possibly still praying for us and working on our behalf. We set aside days to honor them as extraordinary examples of Christian love and commitment, but we do not honor them because they were perfect. In fact, it is their very humanity in all its strengths and weaknesses that causes us to marvel at the miracles they worked or the witness they bore.

This book has focused on the success of Frances Perkins by illuminating the relationship between her theological acumen and her remarkable career, her rich spiritual life and her servant ministry. It has not told the story of those elements of her life that might have been a disappointment to herself or to others. The story of her family relationships seems to be one such area.

For almost half her career, Perkins did not live with her husband. Although the record indicates that they clearly loved each other in the early years of their marriage, Paul Wilson developed a mental illness, now widely understood to have been bipolar disorder. It required his hospitalization during the best years of Perkins' life.

In fact, at the precise moment of her greatest achievement, the signing of the Social Security Act, Perkins was preoccupied with the news received just moments before that her husband's nurse had called to tell her he had disappeared. Immediately after the signing, Perkins took a cab to Union Station and boarded the next train for New York.[61]

With the help of friends, she found him unharmed, but the incident represented the kind of potential calamity that always lurked around the corner of her personal life. The demands of her career and the need to be the breadwinner for the family precluded the kind of close involvement that might have warded off such dangers.

Her relationship with her daughter Susanna was also complicated by Susanna's own struggle with bipolar disorder, serious enough to require hospitalization during her sophomore year at Bryn Mawr.[62]

Her years living with Mary Harriman Rumsey were a major bright spot in her Washington years. With Mary's wealth and flair for entertaining, Perkins was at the center of

Washington's social life. It was also a home where Susanna could visit and join in the fun.

This happy situation, though, came to a sad end. Mary had gone to her farm in Virginia to celebrate her fifty-third birthday with a ride to the hounds. She was thrown from her horse and sustained injuries that ultimately led to her death. On December 19, 1934, she died with her three children, brother Averell Harriman, and the ever-steadfast Frances Perkins at her bedside.

Following the funeral at Mary's parish, St. Thomas, Washington, Perkins and Eleanor Roosevelt accompanied her casket to Arden, New York, where she was buried next to her parents, Mary Averell and E.H. Harriman, in the St. John's churchyard.

A week later, knowing that she was shortly to lose her home, she invited the members of the Committee on Economic Security to sit around the dining room table in the house she had shared with Mary. She locked the door and put a single bottle of whiskey on the table and told them no one was leaving until the Social Security bill was completed. It was.[63]

Just after Christmas, Perkins was tasked with finding a new home, a difficult task under any circumstances, but one complicated by her limited financial resources, which had been severely strained by the cost of care for both her husband and her daughter. It was at that point that newly elected Caroline O'Day suggested they live together. It was a very suitable arrangement, but it too would end sadly when Caroline took ill in early 1942 and died one day after the expiration of her term a year later.

These losses might have been more bearable with the support of a stronger family than the one she actually had. Late in life, she feared that she had been a poor mother she was always off somewhere "saving the world", a notion some who knew her reinforced.[64]

These difficulties are included here not to detract from the image that emerges from the St. Bede Lectures of a holy life sincerely lived. Instead, its inclusion is intended to validate Perkins' own comments about the importance of self-acceptance and self-examination. She appears to have been genuinely aware of many of her shortcomings, which she often catalogued under the "sin of pride", including her fierce commitment to privacy and her treatment of intrusive reporters. The Gospel message embedded in the Bede lectures is that a holy and creative life of service is possible despite personal failings if the individual Christian will genuinely accept the forgiveness God provides.

Mt. Holyoke's Class of 1902, of which Perkins was the president, had adopted the biblical phrase "Be ye steadfast" as its class motto. It is taken from 1 Corinthians 15:58, "Therefore, my beloved brethren, be ye steadfast, unmovable, always abounding in the work of the Lord, forasmuch as ye know that in the Lord your labor is not in vain."

Perkins was indeed steadfast in her life in the church, drawing on its accumulated wisdom and seeking the nurture of the sacraments throughout her adult life. She was also steadfast in her work, overcoming the barriers of a woman in a man's world and establishing safeguards for human life and dignity that remain in place on a national scale to this day.

When her life in both the church and the world is taken into full account, it is possible to see, that, for Perkins, the biblical quotation was more than just the source of a class motto.

It was the story of her life.

I came to Washington to work for God, FDR, and the millions of forgotten, plain, common working men.

—Frances Perkins

Notes

[1] *New York Times*, March 5, 1934, page 1, column 7.

[2] Frank Mason North, "Where Cross the Crowded Ways of Life," *The Hymnal 1940* (New York: The Church Pension Fund, © 1940), Hymn #498.

[3] Frances Perkins, in a letter to Bernard Iddings Bell, Sept. 28, 1944, Columbia University, Rare Book and Manuscript Library, Frances Perkins Papers, Part III.

[4] George Martin, *Madam Secretary* (Boston: Houghton Mifflin Company, 1976).

[5] Herbert Thurston, "Christian Names" in *The Catholic Encyclopedia* 1911. Retrieved March 1, 2018.

[6] Martin., p. 56.

[7] Kirstin Downey, *The Woman Behind the New Deal* (New York: Nan Talese/Doubleday, © 2009), p. 18.

[8] Martin, p. 58.

[9] John Keble's *National Apostasy* sermon, delivered at the University Church of St. Mary the Virgin, Oxford, England, July 14, 1833.

[10] Downey, p. 22.

[11] Martin, pp. 66-67.

[12] James N. Gregory, *The Southern Diaspora: How the Great Migrations of Black and White Southerners Transformed America* (Chapel Hill, NC: University of North Carolina Press, © 2005), p. 330.

[13] Author interview with John Vidumsky of hiddencityphila.org, March 2017.

[14] Martin, p. 67.

[15] Parish records at the Church of the Holy Spirit, Lake Forest, and St. Clement's, Philadelphia, do not establish a transfer of membership; however, occasional references to St. Clement's appear in Perkins' correspondence.

[16] Rexford G. Tugwell, "Some Formative Influences in the Life of Simon Nelson Patten," *The American Economic Review*. Vol XII, N. 1.

Supplement (New Haven, Ct: The American Economic Association), 1922, pp.273-285.

[17] Downey, pp. 67-68.

[18] Maurice Reckitt Papers, University of Sussex Special Collections, Box 19, Folder 2, General Correspondence.

[19] Martin, *Madam Secretary,* p. 238.

[20] Mother Virginia, "The Frances Perkins We Knew" in *Commemorative Booklet: The Frances Perkins Memorial Conference on the Church and Labor Today*, New York: Diocese of New York, © 1995, p. 7.

[21] Harriman, Florence Jaffray (Daisy). *Mission to the North.* Philadelphia: J.B. Lippincott, © 1941, pp. 23-25.

[22] Charles Owen Moore, Jr. "The Frances Perkins We Knew", p. 7.

[23] Brochure announcing the St. Bede Lectures for 1948, Columbia University, Rare Book and Manuscript Library, Frances Perkins Papers—Coggeshall Collections, Box 124.

[24] *New York Times*, Jan. 26, 1948, p. 1.

[25] Unless otherwise cited, all direct quotations of Frances Perkins in this section are taken from "A Christian Order of Society," an unpublished transcript, Columbia University, Rare Book and Manuscript Library, Frances Perkins Papers—Coggeshall Collections. Box 124.

[26] The hymn text says "Judge" rather than "King," but the meaning is essentially the same. It is taken from a poem by the thirteenth century monk, Bernard of Cluny, translated by John Mason Neale in 1851. It appeared as Hymn #39 in the *Hymnal 1940* and under different numbers in predecessor hymnals.

[27] She may be referring to the *Christian News-Letter*, which was published in London by the Council on the Christian Faith and Common Life in the early 1940s. The Scottish missionary, Joseph Houldsworth Oldham, was the editor.

[28] "Thousands Get Oil as City Observes Check on Trucks," *New York Times*, Feb. 2, 1948, p. 1.

[29] "Hydrants Blocked, Fire Takes Four Lives," ibid.

[30] "William O'Dwyer," *Current Biography 1941* (New York: The H.W. Wilson Company), p. 631.

[31] Unless otherwise cited, all direct quotations of Frances Perkins in this section are taken from "The Vocation of the Laity," an unpublished transcript, Columbia University, Rare Book and Manuscript Library, Frances Perkins Papers—Coggeshall Collections. Box 124.

[32] Letter to Bernard Iddings Bell, July 1, 1943, Columbia University, Rare Book and Manuscript Library, Frances Perkins Papers, Part III.

[33] Perkins, draft book review, p. 4, Columbia University, Rare Book and Manuscript Library, Frances Perkins Papers. Box 58.

[34] For more on theology behind the coronation liturgy, see Ian Bradley, *God Save the Queen: The Spiritual Dimension of Monarchy* (London: Continuum International Publishing Group) © 2012.

[35] *A Christian Realm*, (Westminster, England: Church Union, 1940), p. 5, Columbia University, Rare Book and Manuscript Library, Frances Perkins Papers—Coggeshall Collections. Box 124.

[36] Perkins, address before the Personnel Research Association, undated, Columbia University, Rare Book and Manuscript Library, Frances Perkins Papers. Box 54.

[37] Perkins, in a speech before the National Consumers' League, New York, Dec. 19, 1949, p. 5, Columbia University, Rare Book and Manuscript Library, Frances Perkins Papers. Box 58.

[38] Ibid., pp. 3-4.

[39] These ideas are among the recommendations found in Maurice B. Reckitt, *The Social Teachings of the Sacraments, being the report of the second Anglo-Catholic Summer School of Sociology, held at Keble College, Oxford, July 1926.* Perkins is believed to have been a participant.

[40] "Match Patent Ended for Humanity's Sake," *New York Times*, January 29, 1911, p. 1.

[41] That is, a "platitude" or a "cliché".

[42] "Imagetive" is the word that actually appears on p. 14 of the transcript of the second lecture. Perkins distinguishes it from "imagination."

[43] Two plays by George Bernard Shaw, the first dealing with slumlords and the second with prostitution.

[44] "Pope Calls for Ban on Atom Bomb as 'Most Terrible' Weapon", *The New York Times,* Feb. 9, 1948, p. 1.

[45] Author interview with the Rev. Charles Owen Moore, Philadelphia, Jan. 17, 1986.

[46] Pamela Darling, "Gift for an Agonized World: Women, Men, and Movements for Social Justice in the Episcopal Church, 1887-1919", unpublished thesis, Keller Library, The General Theological Seminary, 1987, *passim.*

[47] Vida Scudder, "Malvern 1941", *The Living Church* (June 14, 1942).

[48] Ibid.

[49] *A Christian Realm*, p 3.

[50] George Wharton Pepper, *Four Convention Addresses*, October 1913.

[51] *A Christian Realm*, p 3.

[52] W.G. Peck, *The Social Implications of the Oxford Movement* (New York: Charles Scribner's Sons, 1933), p. 244.

[53] Ibid., pp. 245-246.

[54] Geoffrey Rowell, *The Vision Glorious* (New York: Oxford University Press, © 1983), p. 242

[55] Scudder, "Malvern 1941".
[56] Maurice B. Reckitt, *Faith and Society* (New York: Longmans, Green and Co., 1932), p. 188.
[57] Ibid., p. 226.
[58] Perkins, National Consumers' League speech, p. 13.
[59] Pierre Lecomte du Noüy, *Human Destiny* (New York: Longman, Green and Co., 1947).
[60] Ibid.
[61] Martin, p. 356.
[62] Downey, p. 250.
[63] Martin, p. 53.
[64] Downey, pp. 380-381.

Bibliography

A Christian Realm, (Westminster, England: Church Union, 1940), p. 5, Columbia University, Rare Book and Manuscript Library, Frances Perkins Papers—Coggeshall Collections. Box 124.

Author interview with John Vidumsky of hiddencityphila.org, March 2017.

Author interview with the Rev. Charles Owen Moore, Philadelphia, Jan. 17, 1986.

Bradley, Ian. *God Save the Queen: The Spiritual Dimension of Monarchy* (London: Continuum International Publishing Group) © 2012.

Brochure announcing the St. Bede Lectures for 1948, Columbia University, Rare Book and Manuscript Library, Frances Perkins Papers—Coggeshall Collections, Box 124.

Commemorative Booklet: The Frances Perkins Memorial Conference on the Church and Labor Today, New York: Diocese of New York, © 1995.

Current Biography 1941 (New York: The H.W. Wilson Company), p. 631.

Darling, Pamela. "Gift for an Agonized World: Women, Men, and Movements for Social Justice in the Episcopal Church, 1887-1919", unpublished thesis, Keller Library, The General Theological Seminary, 1987, *passim.*

Downey, Kirstin. *The Woman Behind the New Deal* (New York: Nan Talese/Doubleday, © 2009).

Gregory, James N. *The Southern Diaspora: How the Great Migrations of Black and White Southerners Transformed America* (Chapel Hill, NC: University of North Carolina Press, © 2005).

Harriman, Florence Jaffray (Daisy). *Mission to the North.* Philadelphia: J.B. Lippincott, © 1941.

"Hydrants Blocked, Fire Takes Four Lives," *New York Times*, Feb. 2, 1948, p. 1.

Keble, John. *National Apostasy* (sermon delivered at the University Church of St. Mary the Virgin, Oxford, England, July 14, 1833).

Lecomte du Noüy, Pierre. *Human Destiny* (New York: Longman, Green and Co., 1947).

Martin, George. *Madam Secretary* (Boston: Houghton Mifflin Company, 1976).

"Match Patent Ended for Humanity's Sake," *New York Times*, January 29, 1911, p. 1.

Maurice Reckitt Papers, University of Sussex Special Collections, Box 19, Folder 2, General Correspondence.

New York Times, Jan. 26, 1948, p. 1.

New York Times, March 5, 1934, page 1, column 7.

North, Frank Mason. "Where Cross the Crowded Ways of Life," *The Hymnal 1940* (New York: The Church Pension Fund, © 1940), Hymn #498.

Peck, W.G. *The Social Implications of the Oxford Movement* (New York: Charles Scribner's Sons, 1933), p. 244.

Pepper, George Wharton. *Four Convention Addresses*, October 1913.

Perkins, Frances, in a letter to Bernard Iddings Bell, Sept. 28, 1944, Columbia University, Rare Book and Manuscript Library, Frances Perkins Papers, Part III.

_____. "A Christian Order of Society," an unpublished transcript, Columbia University, Rare Book and Manuscript Library, Frances Perkins Papers—Coggeshall Collections. Box 124.

_____. Address before the Personnel Research Association, undated, Columbia University, Rare Book and Manuscript Library, Frances Perkins Papers. Box 54.

_____. Draft book review, p. 4, Columbia University, Rare Book and Manuscript Library, Frances Perkins Papers. Box 58.

_____. Letter to Bernard Iddings Bell, July 1, 1943, Columbia University, Rare Book and Manuscript Library, Frances Perkins Papers, Part III.

_____. Speech before the National Consumers' League, New York, Dec. 19, 1949, p. 5, Columbia University, Rare Book and Manuscript Library, Frances Perkins Papers. Box 58.

"Pope Calls for Ban on Atom Bomb as 'Most Terrible' Weapon", *The New York Times,* Feb. 9, 1948, p. 1.

Reckitt, Maurice B. *Faith and Society* (New York: Longmans, Green and Co., 1932), p. 188.

_____. *The Social Teachings of the Sacraments, being the report of the second Anglo-Catholic Summer School of Sociology, held at Keble College, Oxford, July 1926.*

Rowell, Geoffrey. *The Vision Glorious* (New York: Oxford University Press, © 1983), p. 242

Scudder, Vida. "Malvern 1941", *The Living Church* (June 14, 1942).

Thurston, Herbert. "Christian Names" in *The Catholic Encyclopedia* 1911. Retrieved March 1, 2018.

"Thousands Get Oil as City Observes Check on Trucks," *New York Times*, Feb. 2, 1948, p. 1.

Tugwell, Rexford G. "Some Formative Influences in the Life of Simon Nelson Patten," *The American Economic Review*. Vol XII, N. 1. Supplement (New Haven, Ct: The American Economic Association), 1922, pp.273-285.